Storyteller on a Sacred Journey

A Collection of Talks and Stories

by Emily B. Boardman

2012-2021

Self-published online with KindleDirect

March 2022

Available at Amazon Books for $10.00

ISBN 9798 4215 40212

eboardman@sbcglobal.net

or

eboardman3@comcast.net

Preface

Emily Boardman was a gentle and modest woman who devoted her life to the well-being of others. In her primary and extended families, in schools, court programs, an AIDS residential hospice and related political organizations, Emily focused her life on justice and support for people on the margins of America's white-privileged society.

After she stopped working for money, Emily trained as an ordained minister but called herself simply a storyteller, one who had always been on a sacred journey. She spoke at the Seminary several times, then brought some of her best stories to the Unitarian Universalist Fellowship in Middletown, New York, between 2013 and 2021. She was always modest about her wisdom and insights, saying she had learned from Native Peoples to "be as a hollow bone," getting ego out of the way so that useful ideas and graceful words could flow through her.

Shortly before her death from a brain tumor at age 76, Emily worked with a few of her many admirers on putting together this collection of some of her stories and presentations. These have not been judged in any way; they are not necessarily "the best."

Emily spoke at the Middletown UU Fellowship more than a hundred times; these are some of the talks we were able to retrieve from her phone and laptop.

Special thanks go to her daughter Amie Saulnier and her son Kilin Boardman-Shroyer; to Rev. Lawrence Schwartz, an early friend from the All-Faiths Seminary International in Manhattan; to Judith Adel and her husband of the Middletown UU Fellowship; and to Joanna Diermeier, a long-time family friend. The cover photo was probably taken during a Two Row event in 2016.

Confined to the written word in this way, Emily's spirit doesn't shine quite as we knew it in person, and of course we can't hear the appreciative sounds from an audience in the background. But even here, Emily's unique style, her insight and her generosity are evident.

Omissions are inevitable in a collection of this sort, unfortunately. For any other errors, I as editor and compiler take responsibility. I am Emily's older sister and was much aided in this project by my partner, Barbara Tye.

Elizabeth F. Boardman   March 2022

Table of Contents

Presentation at All Faiths Seminary International (AFSI), 2013

Standing By at the End: Being Present with the Dying

(We transcribed this talk from a video and an auto-recorder as best we could.)

Today I was asked to do a little bit of a talk on my experience of being with those at the end of life, those who are dying. That's a very wonderful subject for me, but it has been sort of strange to be putting this together during the last month, just as I have been spending a lot of time with little people coming into the world. I've been with three people who have delivered very high-risk babies, and one woman who is trying to keep her legs closed until tomorrow, until Monday, so that I can get up there.

But what I discovered is that these transitions into the world and out of the world are very similar. What is required when you are privileged to be able to have that place, be in that place, is just to hold the space. There's very little you can do. There's nothing magic, there's nothing remarkable, you're just sharing the space for a pretty momentous occasion.

So before I even go any further, I want you to really think about yourselves at those moments when you learn a lot, when you are open, you are fully receptive, where you're integrated, where you know that there is something very special that is happening,

I want to start with three short stories.

I have been with I think twenty-seven people who have died. Those twenty-seven are people who are more etched into my mind and heart than even my own children, even more than the great loves of my life. I wouldn't say that I understand fully why that is, except that perhaps when people are dying, they let go of ego, and when people let go of ego, they suddenly become fully who they are.

So when you move beyond ego, the question is, how do we know how to interact, how do we know how to socially interact with one another. I think that the lessons that I've learned are primarily about that: who we are when we recognize that we are being called to be fully who we are; and how we know to move beyond ego.

So, Russell. Let me tell you about Russell. I knew him so well; I knew him probably better than anybody else knew him. He had shared with me who he was in ways I had never expected a person to share with me, the depths of, and the many layers of, who they were.

When Russell was in the hospital, I came in one day and the head nurse said, Who is she? What is she doing here? I do not understand her place in your life. And he said, This is my spiritual wife. I gasped, Why did you say that? And he said, Isn't that what this is all about?

So I am talking about a kind of intimacy that goes beyond bodily intimacy. I'm talking about knowing each other without the ego. I'm talking about knowing beyond judgement. I'm talking about being open and receptive without a personal agenda. When people are dying, it's very clear that they don't need judgement anymore. It's over, folks. It's useless. You can't fix them. You can't correct them. There are no solutions in your hands, and you gotta let that stuff down. Just go and drop it, quick, because it has no place at that moment of transition.

Russell had shared with me his hopes, his fears, his sins and we had just gotten beyond those as obstacles, so that they had nothing to do with him. I think when you are with people who are dying, sins are totally irrelevant. When all the family is talking about how "that guy messed us over", it's totally irrelevant, it has no more bearing. Dying people are no longer concerned with our little social and personality issues and squabbles.

One day Russell called me and said, I need to go fishing and I said, Oh, ahh…thinking quickly to myself how to do it.

(I did all these things for people when they were dying. I loved following their directions when they were dying, because they thought of some of the most creative things.)

So I immediately thought, I can get the van down and I can put down the seats and I could drive the van out to the shore and he could go fishing.

Oh, sure, sure, man! The man had 72 hours left, and I was going to get him out fishing!?

But Russell looked at me and said, I could go fishing with my sister and my dad. (I knew they had died years ago.) Or, he said, I could go with my brother and my nephew. Oh, OK, I responded, so who would you like to go with? Well, he said, we wouldn't need to worry about the van or our fishing license if I went with my Dad and my sister. And I said, I guess we wouldn't. He said, I think it doesn't really matter which point on the shore I fish at, and I said, What shore? He said, The shore.

So slowly, I said, The shore that you are going to go to with your Dad and your sister, and the shore that you are going to go to with your brother and your nephew, they are on the same lake. And he said, Em, you know that you know this. ("You know this." He used to say that to me often.) You know this, you know how it is. And I said, I don't. He said, We only think we are not connected. It's the same lake.

So I would ask you to remember that it is the same lake, and there are different places on the shore. I don't claim any knowledge of after life, so I don't want to go there. But I certainly have been very, very comforted by what many people have shared at the end of their lives.

The second story is this. I was a recipient of the AIDS Institute Award because of this community residence that I started for people living with AIDS, because I thought they had a right to a place to die with dignity. So I went forward to receive this award, and the

Commissioner whispered, without any congratulations, We don't even fund your program, but there were so many testimonials we couldn't deny you this recognition.

Now I was supposed to have a speech to say when I was receiving this award for the community residence. Well, I was flabbergasted, I had no idea what to say. I accepted the award and sat down. And afterwards they asked me to go upstairs to a classroom where people shared their testimonials.

Now, "testimonials" – that could suggest that I doing these great and wonderful things, well, they weren't so terrific. People, one after another, kept saying, Well, she did this and she did that, and she was able to do this and then she did that. But it was just ho-hum kinds of things. It wasn't remarkable. It wasn't unnecessarily generous. And I really did not understand what all this meant.

But one man, who I had only seen once, he said, There were no conditions attached to what she gave.

And I got it. I just got it. I got it that when you are standing by -- whatever the transition is, and you are standing by, there can be no attachment. You're not there because you're going to get into heaven. You're not there because the family is going to be impressed.

You're not there because you're going to feel better about yourself. You're there just to witness and honor the transition that's happening.

It's the same with all this baby stuff. I was telling someone just a couple of weeks ago: I just am trying to be present.

My daughter said, Mom, I thought when you got here, you'd be able to do something awesome, make this different. But I said, I can't, I can't. And I thought to myself, Oh, what am I doing here? I mean WHAT am I doing here? And then I remembered, Oh yeah, I'm just going to hold the space. I'm just going to try to stand beyond my own agenda, my own needs, her agenda, and the hospital's agenda, whatever.

There's the story of my mother. Finally, my mother was dying, and my siblings thought it was strange that my mother would have me there with her because she had had a lot of trouble with me. Of her six children, she really had trouble with me. But there I was at the time of her death.

Remember, if you are asked to be there at the time of somebody's dying, it's because you can do it. It has nothing to do with anything else. It's because you can be there, and you will rise to the occasion.

Listening to our mother, my sisters kept saying it was incoherent rambling, that I was trying to make sense out of incoherent rambling.

I would suggest that many of us have missed the golden opportunity of being with those who are dying because we thought that their words were incoherent rambling. It doesn't matter what is being said, if you stop to listen, you may find it is not incoherent.

At one point, my mother said to me, There's a vehicular contraption here to pick me up. Vehicular contraption? Yes, she nods, and says, Oh, you're the one who can't spell, that's right. So she spelled out VEHICULAR and drew a picture in the air, saying, Look at that, just look at it. I said, You know that not only can I not spell, but I also can't see. She said, You just put your head here on this pillow and look at what's in front of you. And she illustrated beautifully — I could even see the little round light bulbs, I could see the running board. I could see exactly what she saw.

So I said to this woman, this elegant Victorian, this embattled woman, I said, Do you think that they're here for you? She said, Well, I don't know, but I would never go anywhere I wasn't wanted.

I didn't know where to go or what to say. So I said, Perhaps if you knocked, it would be opened. She turned and looked at me (although at that point she was never looking, she was never seeing me) and she said, Oh, Emmy, I am a seeker, a seeker. And I said, Perhaps you have been found. She said, I wish it were so, but not yet, and drifted off into a place where I couldn't follow her.

Of all the hundreds of stories that I have to share with you about dying, I thought to myself, why would I share these stories on this day? It is because the name of this walk is *Standing by at the End of Life*.

I would suggest that first of all, Russell is right. We do know a lot about dying. We know a lot about letting go. We know about losing things that are treasures, and about having to let go of things and move on to other things.

I think Russell is right in saying that I could feel my heart beating when he was talking about the lake. I could feel myself thinking, I'm not big enough or evolved enough to be able to have this information. I think that not only could I not spell vehicular contraption but a part of me couldn't believe that there was a vehicular contraption that was there to pick her up.

Yet a part of me knew that, yes, we create our lives, and we create our deaths and her agenda, her personal beliefs, her personal history kept playing out right up to the very end. I've seen that again and again and again, the way you live is the way you die. Practice dying every time you have the opportunity.

They never, nothing, nobody has ever described a terrifying place to me when they talked about dying. Nobody ever. Never. It's all been quite familiar, and it was just me who was on this side of the veil. I couldn't see what was just on the other side. But they weren't alarmed. They assumed that I understood. They assumed I could see the vehicular contraption. They assumed that I knew about the lake. They assumed that I understood what the actions were that were worthy of the award.

So we've got to figure out a little bit more about who we are as the essential selves, because the essential self is the person who is called for when standing by at the end of life for another person.

The idea of having a special gift, I don't know that it really is a special gift, it's just simply, I think it's just about being present. And I think that very often we don't know what present means. What does it mean to be present? It means perhaps to have no expectations. You don't know what you are going to do.

One man testified that I had given him my cell phone at Christmas time because I was leaving him in the hospital and he wasn't going to be connected to anybody, while I have so many. And this man was going to die if he didn't have some way to connect to something. I asked him, Tracy, are you ready to die? He said, Why am I here? I said, I don't really know, but if you want to stay, perhaps you'll need a cell phone. So I gave him the cell phone and in his testimonial, he describes that cell phone as really a link to God.

Another young woman told how I had come to see her when she was very sick and alone with four children. I stopped and bought a chicken and some collard greens before I went to see her, and I put the greens and chicken on the stove. And in her testimonial, she said, She came to help me die and fed my children first.

So at the end of life, when people are trying to let go, they are looking at us in ways that are very generous and very open-hearted. Now, I only thought I was bringing some chicken and some collard greens, you know just, you know, I knew the situation. But what she saw was that I had come to help her die but fed the children first.

So, remember that the simple mundane way that we do things in the world is transformed, we are transformed by those who see us from that place.

When I first agreed to do this talk last March, I thought, Good Grief, what did I get myself into? Hey, oh, my gosh, why did I do this? Who do I think I am? What do I think I'm doing? How am I going to do this? These people are totally unrealistic. Now they're going to talk about the retreat on top of everything else? And I've still got sixteen papers to write!

And there was a whole lot of stuff that had been kicked up for me, a whole lot of stuff. I was real disappointed in religion. I was real disappointed what we had done in the name of religion. I felt very personally betrayed and I felt very personally adrift.

So, I remembered that Hindu king story, you know. It offered a bit of perspective.

It's the story of a saddhu and a man who was a king in India, in a northern Indian community. He had six castles, five cars and he had six children. They had all been raised. He had made a fortune in India and he came to this country to see one of his sons, who was at Tufts University. He saw an uncle of his somewhere in his family who was a saddhu here in this country.

He said, I am a king. I have more wealth and power in India than almost anybody else. Why am I so unhappy? And the story that was shared here earlier was absolutely to the point. Because you have seen how unhappy the world is.

So, he said, What do I do now that I have all the power and I have all the riches and I have all the things that the world has to offer. What do I do to find happiness? And his teacher said, You pick up your bowl and walk. But, he said, I am a King! The uncle said, So you can't walk in India and you can't walk in Europe. But you had better find a place to pick up your bowl and walk, because there is much you need to let go of before you have to die. You've got a great deal of work ahead of you.

So he went to Venezuela, where he didn't speak the language, where nobody knew he came from India, yeah, no one knew him from Adam, probably. And that's where he took up his bowl and that's where he walked.

Actually, I met him at the ashram – it's quite a wonderful place to go to – I don't need to tell you. And he told me at the ashram that the reason he needed to come to the Americas was, we didn't know that we all die. He said that Westerners have very little concept that they die, and that they are really quite demented in their inability to understand that we all leave this world at some point.

I can remember going back and looking it up and seeing that the Hindus have four quarters for a lifetime. The first one is to look and take on the world; then the second is to be the householder. The third is to have to begin to give up all the trappings of the world; and you are very relieved and very reassured to be able to give up the trappings of the world, the trappings of the institutions, trappings of religion, trappings of the family.

But the fourth quarter is where you also have to give up the things that you love.

So I would say, just in closing, that one of the things that is very important to really respect when you are with those people at the end of life and their families is that they are giving up not only----if they haven't done the prior work of dying---they are giving up a lot of stuff, but they are also having to give up what they've only just discovered that they love. Again and again and again, people have told me how just barely, you know, just the last week of life, they discovered what they loved, they discovered who they loved, they discovered what they wanted for that person, for that thing, for that part of themselves. It was only at that last moment, because we are so unpracticed, because we are so unconscious about the passage of dying that we are totally unprepared for what is such a holy instant. To be there when somebody takes that last breath is a moment to be eternally grateful for.

I have a great deal of respect for the body and for the world, and we abuse them both, the world and the body. But we know them to be the greatest comforter and the greatest source of our being. When you are invited to be there with somebody at the end of their lives, just know you are very blessed that you are given the opportunity to embrace another person on the soul level. There is nothing more special.

Excerpts from presentations at the Unitarian Universalist Fellowship in Middletown, New York.

Born Again

Easter 2015

Reuben was in seventh grade, lonely and disconnected. His parents were undocumented restaurant workers who lived in fear. I once asked Reuben where he lived and he actually said, "I live in Fear." They were particularly fearful that Reuben's being in school would expose them. He was their only child and as much as they loved him, they believed he put them at risk. He told me that he was twelve and had never been good at anything and had never been useful and that there was no reason for him to be alive. Nothing I could say or do helped. He was in trouble and suicidal, but told me, his counselor, that he would deny everything if I called the officials.

Easter break was around the corner and I battled with my apprehension that Reuben would take his life during the school holiday. It was the Thursday before the break when I saw on the absentee sheet that Reuben was not in school. My last chance to intervene was past.

But at 9, in the morning, I heard footsteps running down the hall and a hot but excited Reuben burst into my office. His face was not the usual scowl but almost radiant. He burst out, "I was useful!"

He proceeded to tell me that he had skipped school and was not sure where or what he was going to do. He knew the truant officer would be looking for him and he was cutting across the Caldor parking lot when suddenly he saw an old woman pushing a cart and a car backing out at the same moment. He knew instantly why he was alive. He darted past another car and, in the nick of time, came up behind the old woman and pushed her up onto the cart handle and all three out of the way of the car within seconds of an accident. He wasn't big, he wasn't strong, he wasn't smart, but HE had saved a life, two lives.

He rarely came to see me after that day. He was another person, born again, resurrected. He had been well used, "useful" and he believed. Believed in himself, the

Universe, the mystery, his own goodness and the
goodness of the world.

A simple story but as rich as all and any of the
resurrection stories you might know from your own life.

This Moment Will Never Come Again

October 2021

It is not only the Indigenous who have called for a different perception and practice than that of the Western Judeo-Christian world, but Eastern paths have become increasingly provocative. I want to share a message from my friend, Brenda Shashona .

Brenda is a Rabbi and a Zen practitioner and a teacher. She has spent a lifetime searching for the transcendent truth. Her clarity and balance of the Eastern and Western traditions is born out of her sitting practice.

It feels to me that there is a golden opportunity just now that we may not want to miss. We are quickly reminded with the drop in temperature and the shortened days that we are preparing to pull back into isolation and separation from the natural world again under the shroud of the pandemic and radical climate crisis. We need to count on ourselves to raise up joy, wonder and gratitude. Some would say "we must be the eyes, ears and hands of God," Others would say that in grounding and intention, we can manifest a Wisdom that the western world has not recognized, a powerful and vibrant wisdom known to all living things if we can be there to witness and be a part of it.

Brenda's message:

Many of us feel trapped by having to go through the same activities again and again. The routines of life can seem stifling, and we long for change, adventure and excitement. It seems we need diversion and distraction from the "same, old thing".

However, the heart of Zen Practice is realizing that nothing is ever the same. It's impossible to truly repeat anything. This moment, this step will never come again.

As we go through what seems like the same, ordinary day, each moment is actually different. There are endless surprises and possibilities waiting. Each day is completely unique and fresh. And so is each person, if only we can see them that way.

It is up to us to attend to each activity and person carefully, rather than feel it's just a dull repetition of what happened before. Nothing is dull unless you see it that way.

*When we are alive and awake to each moment,
whatever appears becomes a wonderful door we
can walk through to a an entirely new life.*
☐

There are moments when we can catch a glimmer,
through the glass darkly, of joy, presence, drama,
usefulness, positivity. ...A real gratitude for the gift of
life fills us, and real joy comes from giving it away.

May I share a couple of such moments before asking you
to share one of your own?

- A quiet nap time filled the room with soft
  breathing and light bouncing off the curtains as
  the leaves blew in the breeze. The little boy
  beside me was asleep. I began to breathe with
  him. I let myself feel the gift of him and was so
  grateful to be able to be there with
  him. Moments later, I turned to look at him and
  his eyes were open and he said, "I love you,
  Beeba" and closed his eyes again. It felt like we
  met somewhere between here and there in a smile
  that filled the space of two beings who shared the
  one journey.

- I went to get a flu shot last week on a Friday at 8:30am after putting the boys on the bus. I waited a bit and was invited into the Minute Clinic. After the usual questions and the shot, the nurse asked me what I did. I said I was a grandmother and a retiring "Storyteller" for a small UU Fellowship. She started asking me with great interest how, where and what stories did I tell.

When I said something about others waiting, she smiled and said she had a cancellation, so we could continue to talk about "God" for half an hour! She was from Haiti and a preacher herself, in her fifties. "God is here in this conversation between the two of us, not in heaven, that is a mistake."

We talked about the cry for Unity and for believing in ourselves as the expression of the Divine. That was what kept us "in gospel order." When I mentioned the divide between heart and mind, she said "Both are homes of the spirit, but without the unity, neither can be trusted."

We agreed that the flu shot had served its purpose.

Every moment serves its purpose if we are there for it.

The meaning of life is to find your gift. The purpose is to give it away.

Pablo Picasso

Grandparents' Day

September 11, 2021

The strange irony is that this traumatic date, 9/11, is also the day set aside to celebrate grandparents of the past, the present and the future. Today I would like to look at the world from the perspective of such a grandparent. Many of us, having reached the culmination of duty and power, look back in order to find hope, to look forward.

- Some of us feel fortunate to tumble forward into a new world with those who will inherit it.
- Some of us watch from the sidelines.
- Some in the midst of the fray are hard pressed to see the forest from the trees.
- Some wish we had done more.
- Some are grateful that they have left no descendants to suffer the consequences ahead.
- Some don't think they got what they "deserved".
- Some of us are grateful to be here with hopeful children.

All of us might feel grateful for all we have been given, and grateful to have witnessed changes for better and/or for worse. We are glad to know that this is about as good as it gets in a world that must change to survive.

I am a little incredulous to realize that almost all my heroes, gurus, teachers, lovers, musicians, actors, role models and many of my dearest friends are dead. I imagine their presence and understand their having moved on.

A Facebook question asks if I have known anyone for more than twenty years. There are few anymore that I have known for less than twenty years.

Except grandchildren. They bring it all home with poignancy and wonderful wisdom, resilience and ambivalent confidence. Sebastian Hope at two and a half is the expression of pure joy, hope and only occasional outrage as I watch him take on the world.

"Oh, Beeba, God means Quiet," says four-year old Sadie, as if my asking the question "What does God mean?" is ridiculous.

There is extraordinary courage, tenacity and compassion out there and I stand in awe. I recognize the entitlement that allows me to feel beyond my own privilege. Not affluence---I only now realize how little money I have made---but permission to think that what I did in the world mattered, if not for thousands, for some. That made me rich with love that has filled my life.

A wise one teaches the "the one who plants trees, knowing that he will never sit in their shade, has at least started to understand the meaning of life."

The Labyrinth Symbol

Jan 8, 2021

A labyrinth is an ancient symbol of wholeness. The imagery of the circle and spiral combine into a meandering but purposeful pattern. The labyrinth represents a journey or path to our own center and back again out into the world.

Labyrinths have long been used as meditation and prayer tools. When we walk one, it serves as a metaphor for life's journey. It is a symbol that creates a sacred space and place and takes us out of our ego to our spirit, to "That Which Is Within."

Four Laws are found within Native American spiritualism

1. The person you meet is the right one.
   No one comes into our lives by accident,
   All the people around us who interact

with us stand for something, either to
educate us or to help us in our situation.

2. What happens is what had to happen.
   When you understand this, you
   confidently look at what's happening,
   thankful for what was there and happy for
   what is going to happen so we can learn
   our lessons to get ahead...

3. Every moment that something begins is the right moment.
   Everything starts at the right time, not
   sooner or later. When we are ready for
   something new in our life, it's already
   there to begin with.

4. What's over is over.
   It's that simple. When something ends in
   our life, it serves our development. That's
   why it's better to let go and move
   forward, [blessed by] the experiences that
   have been gained.

I don't think it is a coincidence that you are reading this here. If this text meets you today, it's because you meet the conditions and understand that no rain drop anywhere accidently falls in the wrong place.

St. Teresa of Avila offered guidance from the Christian tradition:

> *Christ has no body but yours, no hand, no feet on earth but yours.*
> *Yours are the eyes with which he looks with compassion on this world.*
> *Yours are the feet with which he walks to do good.*
> *Yours are the hands with which he blesses all he world.*
> *Christ has no body now on earth but yours.*

A main principle of Zen philosophy is the denial of the ego, the focus on interconnectedness in the universe, the recognition of attachment as a source of suffering, and the realization that human perception is faulty.

> Let it go well.
> Love with your whole being.
> Be happy without end.

Every day is a happy day.
We Are Oneness.

The Cosmic Dancer

Do not ask your children
to strive for extraordinary lives.
Such striving may seem admirable,
but it is the way of foolishness.
Help them instead to find the wonder
and the marvel of an ordinary life.
Show them the joy of tasting
tomatoes, apples, and pears.
Show them how to cry
when pets and people die.
Show them the infinite pleasure
in the touch of a hand.
And make the ordinary come alive for them.
The extraordinary will take care of itself.

~William Martin

Pain

February 2021

For most of us white owning-class folks, pain is not the biggest part of the puzzle of life, but it is a significant fraction. I ask us to first look at what pain is for us and how we have come to make room for it, learn from it and share it.

Maya Angelou tells us:

> *Pain is the teacher of the most significant lessons. Pain breaks you open. Pain opens the third eye. Pain identifies the intersections of our lives. Pain wakes us up and reminds us of what matters. Pain exposes the one behind the curtain. Pain is the confrontation with self-picture. Pain brings you to your knees. Pain calls you forward and shows you who you can be, what you can endure, what you can rise from.*
>
> > *From Still I Rise.*

[Whether we suffer from physical or emotional pain,] often we don't look at the resulting outcome of that pain. We rush past it and only if we are lucky, do we pause and see the guiding hand of change helping us to become more realized.

Those who do see the intersections, the place where that painful agent of change takes hold, might see the necessity of such a hand to shake us awake, or pull us onto a course we would not take willingly.

Those I know who have embraced the lessons of the change agent of pain have a respect and tolerance for pain that is not exacerbated by shame, guilt or blame....

Review the labyrinth of your life and look at the points of pain, anguish, loss. Look at how the trajectory of your life felt altered. Look at the acquired strength of character that was born in that moment and at the you you knew was no longer who you were.

The Gift of Gratitude

December 2017

I have been thinking of the gifts that my mother gave me in her frustrated efforts to rein me in. My sister would say they were "punishments" or "discipline for an unruly child" and I confess there were times when it felt that way.

I was an excitable and agitated little girl. I was not interested in what was on the blackboard, but in what was happening in the lives of those around me both in and outside the classroom. What was the bird doing, what socks were kids wearing, what was the scratch on the teacher's arm caused by, who had lunch and who didn't and why? My heart dragged me around by the nose. Too many animals and dolls filled my bed, so I slept on the floor. My family called me "Fairy Fey" or the "Odd One."

I always felt loved even if disapproved of and constantly corrected by my brilliant, capable, confident mother who had to work hard, and often ineffectually, to keep me in line.

My father's love was unconditional and that gave me the ground on which I stand, the courage to "expect a miracle," the sensitivity to "drive to the comfort of my passengers," and the grace to dance as if no one was watching. He gave me the best that I am.

Trinity

October 2018

If we choose fear, we will find it. If we choose hope, we will find it. The self-serving definition of hope is looking for personal gratification, but the older and much less common meaning of hope is about trusting life without expectation of attaining any particular outcome any time soon. This type of hope has a quiet but unshakable faith in whatever happens and in the human capacity to respond to it constructively. It is a positive but not necessarily optimistic attitude to life that does not depend on external conditions or circumstances.

Bobby McLeod, Maori elder

If we look for the good in All Good, we understand we need to try to understand the bad and the ugly that comes with it. ...

I want to bring us back still further and consider the trinity of the Original Instructions: the Sky, the Earth and the Water.

Is the Sky not the source of all the properties of life; the Earth she who received the seed; and the Water the miracle substance that brings life into being and sustains it?

> *To heal ourselves, we must heal our planet, and to heal our planet we must heal ourselves.* - Bobby McLeod

Look at the sacred triangle of your three-legged stool and know that:

> *"What you do makes a difference, and you have to decide what kind of difference you want to make."* - Jane Goodall

Acceptance and Encouragement

July 2021

Acceptance and encouragement are essential.

> *Spiritual growth isn't about a vertical ascent to heaven but about growth in every dimension at once. It's spirituality in 3-D. Growth in spirit doesn't measure one's proximity to a God above, but rather the spaciousness of one's own soul— its volume, its capacity, its size.*
> *We need souls that can take in the world in all its complexity and diversity, yet still maintain our integrity. And we need souls that can love and be in relationship with all of this complexity. Instead of fight or flight, we need a spiritual posture of embrace.*
>
> Rev. Rob Hardies, All Souls Church Unitarian, Washington, DC

I thought this might be a good guidance to lead us forward into the very murky future..... My own good fortune is to be spending time with children who keep me smiling and pulling my focus back to what is. The placement of ourselves as part of a continuum of generations helps us to appreciate the broad and deep ways in which we can accept and encourage a particular person.

Many of us at some point look to a spiritual/faith tradition to join, a place where we can trust that acceptance and encouragement will transcend the petty friction and stress of insecurity and the bombardment of the dominant cultures.

I believe there is only one life per person and one opportunity to get it right. We need one another to share the wonder and awe of this brief visit; just sharing that knowledge will embolden each of us. We are all children taking on the world and slowly letting it go.

We have all said, What's it all about? and sometimes Why bother? We have all stopped and considered the tear-stained cheek of a child and said, This is worth caring for. We have all stood up after being tripped or thrown down.

We can all look at the essential tools of our backpack and be grateful that acceptance and encouragement are always available to us. We have all come to know them in our lifetime and know that they have served us well, both in their being given and being received. ...

Let us remember that on Sunday here at UU, we refuel, re-member, re connect. We accept and encourage one another to believe in the most loving and courageous of who we are....

I ask us to all remember these words:

> *I shall pass through this world but once. Any good therefore that I can do or any kindness that I can show to any human being, let me do it now. Let me not defer or neglect it, for I shall not pass this way again.*
>
> Quaker Stephen Grellet

Precepts change and being right isn't as important as being kind, being rich isn't the path to happiness, and being wrong may mean you're right.

Flowering Night Cereus

September 2019

Raggedy, long, gangling, inflexible stalk-like leaves
grow three feet out into the room with unbridled
lankiness. In short, a most unattractive plant in the cactus
family which has filled my bedroom window for twenty
years. In the summer, I would put it outside where the
leaves would burn and crack. The promise that this most
beautiful of flowers would bloom for four hours in one
night a year would elude me, year after year.

As I prepared to go north to Massachusetts, I wondered
if it was worth taking this cactus even further beyond its
natural habitat, but I couldn't imagine to whom I could
bequeath such an ungainly albatross. I left it to survive
my absence.

After six weeks away, I came home after a hot spell to
find not one but two buds on the plant that had been left
on the porch with little or no care imposed by mere
mortals.

I quickly researched the time it would take to bloom.

The trick here is that this miracle happens in the dark of the night (between 9 and 11pm). The blooms last only four hours.

They are 9" in diameter with rich pink/orange/beige exterior petals that open to reveal three layers of pure white crepe-thin petals. There is a stigma of three, then an additional three prongs that suddenly become nine, in a bed of stamens that spring up, tossing the pollen out onto the petals for easy access for the one moth who comes to retrieve it. As the pollen is released, a very strong, pungent, vanilla-sweet essence is released that can be smelt, it is said, for up to a mile or more. Bats are drawn by the smell in hopes of catching the moths that come for the pollen.

I was delighted by the buds and invited a half a dozen friends to expect my call at the Great Moment, some night soon.

But then I had to leave for DC for a last visit with grandchildren before the start of school. Clearly this 4ft wide, 3ft long happening would have to go with me.

In DC, we planned a gathering, but again, the nights passed but nothing happened. It was time to go on to a niece who is struggling with a terminal condition in Western Pennsylvania, and again I packed up the plant.

I arrived at 3 in the afternoon, and as the children prepared for bed, I went to check on the plant, and yes, it was starting!

We gathered together and watched the petals opening in the quiet dark of the porch. Ben and I stayed with it, Ben taking pictures and me grateful for the moment, and for the place of this miracle…. My niece and I, who had talked about her "bucket list" only hours earlier, smiled at one another, grateful to have shared this moment.

The hidden gift of this unique plant is such a powerful and poignant expression of the miracle of which we are a part. I return home to the little house at the base of Sugar Loaf Mountain and reflect on the wonders of the Great Web.

Here before me, the dahlias flower and the butterflies dance across them, the iridescent wings of the dragonflies catch the light, the wings of the honey-bees hum, and the cardinal's song rises above the cicadas. The backdrop is the lush green solidity of great trees who know their source and reach into blue skies full of light and warmth.

As we push the limits of our provider and sustainer, indeed, our very source, may we take the time to pay homage and express gratitude to the Web of Life.

What Is the Gift?

December 24, 2014

Christmas as a story that shows a miraculous birth has precedents as far back as when the story of the birthing of the sun was told, thousands of years before the story of Mary and Joseph.

People all over the world have always noted the increasing darkness of the winter season and created stories and myths that would ward off that fearful loss of light and warmth. The longest day of the year weighed heavy and the promise of the return of light leant itself to be a ceremonial day of potential and hope. Not to mention that the Winter Solstice was also the time of butchering and the fermentation of wines. And so arises in almost all cultures, a ritual ceremony surrounding the promise of the return of the Sun. It is out of these stories that the story of the nativity arose. Even the immaculate conception comes from a line of immaculate conceptions that predated the Jesus story. It is said there were as many as 72 would-be messiahs.

Some would find it sacrilegious to return our theological "truth" to its more factual grounding, but to me it feels right. That the story of Jesus (the light/warmth/love) should be slipped into such a tradition couldn't be more fitting. What was created was a story that personified the myths of the pagan traditions. Like so much of Catholic ritual, the Christmas story also was built on "pagan" foundations. The power, awe, and mystery were imbedded in the traditional connections to Earth, Sky, Harvest, Water and Spirit (breath) could not be denied when one was trying to introduce a new myth(e)ology.

A friend reminds me of the San Juan Turtle dancers, the line of men with their booming voices and footfalls and their seed rattles (no drum for this most sacred of dances), backs and heads leaning forward, focused together, listening to each other, singing of the connection to earth and inviting (or rather, perhaps, joining) the turning of the light to longer days. The clowns are there, boot laces untied, in loincloths, perhaps cooing to a Santa Claus doll, probably dragging on a cig, then inviting a lady watcher to come and dance the two-step on the plaza, making people laugh and turning everything upside down. This ceremony was outlawed by the Roman Catholics for hundreds of years but revived in 1960.

I remember the Solstice gatherings of years past with singing and dancing to coax the sun to return, and with promises that we would be better children of creation.

I remember the great bonfires in Denmark that were built so that all the regrets and ill-will could be tossed onto the great jule log that gave the very light and warmth that the waning sun had withheld.

Then recently I read that it was a Unitarian minister who was responsible for bringing Christmas forward after the early Protestants had banned it in the old New England.

What is this Christmas story? How does it speak to us, Christians, non-Christians, indeed to the UU interfaith family? I have looked about and asked what UU congregants make of Christmas, but it was a gift from my son that brought another Christmas story home, the one that speaks to us all.

Kilin gave me tickets to see "The Christmas Carol." I was struck again how grounded in community and good will this story is. Dickens does not dwell on Mary and Joseph in a stall, but on a life worth living, past, present and future. We are asked to consider the light we may or may not have brought to a world that shudders in darkness.

"The Christmas Carol" looks at service, justice, integrity, generosity, care and concern for others and reveals them as paths that open us up, free us, and bring us into community. I am reminded of the UU Covenant.

Mr. Marley brings the gift of a heartfelt insight and hindsight. With the light turned first on the hope-filled years of Ebenezer's childhood, to the grasping greed of his midlife, to the blind and sullen view toward all life in his old age, Scrooge is given one last chance to know what he has always known and do what he always wanted to do. The message is simple and direct: it's up to you. Jesus would agree and understand it as a universal truth, a truth that is available to all everywhere.

The Christmas story of Mary and Baby Jesus belongs to each of us. We create it in the lives we live every day. What level of light and love do we bring forward? How selfish and disgruntled are we? Where is our gratitude? How do we practice what we claim to believe? Does a Black Life Matter? Does truth matter? Do I believe that "I will do unto others as I would have them do unto me"?

So I implore us all to give the best that we have to this new beginning! And may *Love bless us, everyone!*

What is Sacred?

Date unknown

The question: What is Sacred? is a question we must each answer for ourselves in the end.

For us new Americans, wonder, awe, joy, tenderness, kindness, reverence, gratitude, atonement, prayer, and more are sign posts that we are coming into a place of the sacred. We pause and recognize (not in sentimentality or obligation) a knowing that we behold and are held in a place, time and space that is by definition sacred.

Many Native Americans, who lived so close to the source and center of their beings, saw it a little differently. I paraphrase Standing Bear of the Teton Sioux:

> *To rail against the storms is an act of futility. Bright days and dark days are both an expression of the Great Mystery and being a part of that great mystery is Sacred. .... Observation is rewarded with wonder, admiration and appreciation for life far beyond mere human forms. Life is vivid and pulsing. Life is Sacred.*

A group of medicine men and priests gathered on the Rosebud Reservation in the late '70s for three years to share the meaning of each ones faith. After three years of attending the group, a medicine man jumped up in frustration and confusion.

Why is it that we are the ones telling you of our experiences of the Spirit, but you remain silent or only refer to the Bible? Why don't you testify to your experiences?

The room was eerily silent.

Why don't we share our experiences of the Spirit, the Sacred? Where is it? What is it? What does it do for us? Do we know it when we see it, feel it, hear it?

Recently I went to the Sun Dance on the Standing Rock Reservation in North Dakota, full of what I hoped was an open receptivity that I trusted would bring me to a place I longed to be. It had been fifty years since I had been there. I had read lots, participated in Inipi lodges, attended ceremonies, and become Clerk of the Indian Affairs Committee of New York Yearly Meeting of Friends (Quakers)... I had taught many classes on Indigenous knowing, and most recently participated in the Two Row.

The opportunity to be at this traditional family Sun Dance came about by my fifty- year friendship with a young woman I had met when I was on the Rosebud Reservation in 1968. She believed that this would be her last dance and wondered if I would come. Of course, and thank you! The dream of a would-be anthropologist would be realized. The Sun Dance is the sacred ceremony at the center of the Lakota World. For many years it was outlawed by the powers of both Church and State. It is back and with it comes a remembering that is important for us all.

The origin story of the Lakota involves the Story of the Rock who gave its own blood to create Father Sky and Mother Earth (mirrored reflections of one another) and *Mitakuye Oyasin*---All our Relations: all who are related, all who participate in the co-creation of life.

The sacrifice of blood that gave birth to the world is still asked of us. Not understanding this will return us to a time when the Great Mother shook us off with great storms, floods, fires and rivers of lava for our selfishness.

Selfishness is believed always to be the cause of our undoing. If one follows the four virtues of the Lakota, selfishness will be kept at bay. They are Wisdom,

Bravery, Fortitude and Generosity. In living those virtues, the sacred and the holy (wholly), a life of grace and connection are found. *Mitakyue Oaysin* is realized.

The Sun Dance is the moment when in the apex of creation between Father Sky and Mother Earth, while tied to the Tree of Life and dancing to the Sun, the dancers go through a realignment of the self, in an act of bravery, fortitude, wisdom and generosity. This is the intention of the sacrifice, not just for the self, but for the world.

To remember our part in the creation is essential to Being. To do otherwise, with a selfish grasping, is to lose our way and forget the connection, to be spun off as unessential, if not dangerous, to our host.

So where is *my* testimonial? Like the priests, I can wax eloquent, but where is the sacred of my own experience? Indeed, the miracle of being at this dance was born of a sustained relationship of fifty years. Indeed, the original miracle was this relationship with a young woman (myself) and an eight-year-old girl who never let me go and knew I would return one day. The wonder of those connections is beyond rhyme or reason. And the third miracle was the willingness to travel through the humiliation of ignorance and ego into humility and receptivity. ...

The Sun Dance was six days full of wonder, awe, joy, kindness, and the wisdom, fortitude and generosity of a sacred ceremony. Who I am today as a story-telling elder on a sacred journey, remembers that young white girl in 1968-1971, open to the wonder of what I didn't understand but trusted. The experiences of that young woman have begun to be understood with the wisdom of hindsight. I have seen the fortitude, bravery and generosity of myself as a young woman and am held in a sacred place of gratitude. The Giveaway they had for me fifty years ago makes sense. The message was given in a spoken language I didn't understand, but it took in the heart. The connection has held. The ties to the tree of life are tests of self and spirit. They are not just painful. The fierceness of the sun is enlightening, not blinding, and the sacrifice of the Buffalo is sacred, and the gift of life itself.

All My Relations [bowing]

What is meant by Interfaith?

Date unknown

The question looms bigger and bigger as the world gets smaller and smaller.

The Pew Report of 2012 is staggering. The institution of religion is imploding. Over a quarter of those under thirty do not identify as "religious" and answer "none" to the question, "What religion do you practice?" There are considerably fewer who bring their families back to the faith tradition of their childhood, and more claim to do yoga and meditation than prayer and church services.

The world is too small and too fragile to sustain the conflicting differences and separateness that the institutions of religion have brought forward. The oneness of this little Blue Marble, this remarkable "pale blue dot" as seen from outer space, is no longer the world of vast and divided continents and oceans. Interviews by the Overview Institute with five astronauts who have seen this amazing little spot in the galaxy from afar, are moving and profound. Each one said that he went out to explore the universe, and saw the Earth, and it changed everything for him, everything. Perhaps it is this quantum leap in perception that finally makes the whole world one. The Kingdom is at hand. The Kingdom is over.

The Dalai Lama says that he came out of Tibet believing that Buddhism was the only path. He met many different faith traditions and understood that there were many paths. Or as Huston Smith says, "There are many paths up the Mountain of Life, but at the top they converge." There are many prophets, but they share a very familiar seed of love and compassion at their core. It does not matter what the story, they are all born out of the same ethical heart of all humans and its capacity to be concerned and connected. It is that which must be remembered.

Perhaps it is the lack of concern and the lack of connection to a world of Love much greater than our self-righteous views of one religion being truer than the other, or more connected than another, that has gotten us in trouble. Our religions can no longer provide the comfort and connection that we so yearn for. It might be that the Monkey Mind, otherwise known as the Egoic Mind, prevents the 'mindfulness' of the eastern traditions that is so crucial to this time of changing paradigms.

Thich Nhat Hanh, a Viet Nam monk, says that we are beings who deeply yearn to be understood, that to be understood is to be loved, and to be loved is to feel free to stop, look and listen. In that deep looking and listening, we discover an opening into a calming, relieving place of joy. In moving from judgement and criticism to compassion and love, we might discover where we are and know that it is good.

And what is that place but the shared fundamental belief of all human beings who live in community: "Do unto others as we would have them do unto us."

In fact, it is this ethical value that all religious prophets/prophecies share, that all religions claim as the corner stone on which their edifices are built, though often forgotten in exclusionary righteousness within their doors.

The years with All Faiths Seminary provided me with a peek into the wonderful potential that lies within the seven great religions. They also revealed the horrific brutality and willingness to exploit of those who were "wrong in the face of their righteousness."

The great contradiction within religion is its very absence of the interfaith understanding and love of which Thich Nhat Hanh speaks. It is the separation from our better selves, our selves that yearn for connection and understanding. . We are ripped asunder as we are excluded because of a failed marriage, a gay son, an "other" in-law, or an evil, pagan, unsaved, other. We are asked to give special consideration to the "priest son", to forgive the rabbi's financial shenanigans, to tolerate the massacre of thousands of Tibetan monks, and to let the Holocaust slide out of the history books, as have so many other historical travesties committed in the name of God.

But wait, let's look again. Let's look at the unique perspective that the religious path has opened for all of us, whatever our religion or tradition, whatever our social strata or level of education. Let us consider the deep yearning for knowing what we cannot know, but often fear like death. What systems of belief have we had access to that have benefited us in that realm of knowing? Consider how much we might benefit from the vast amount of work that the eastern traditions have brought to learning to walk toward death with equanimity and honor. (Aygen Rimpoche)

Consider the generosity and courage of the Catholic Worker, and the service work provided by so many good and loving people from every religion in the face of both national and natural travesties and traumas with concern and a sense of connection as the impulse. Stop and ask yourself if the stories of your faith tradition aren't fundamental to your ethical code. Has that innate knowing of the mysteries of life been given confirmation and affirmation in your faith tradition?

Yes, there are many failings and much that needs to be dismantled but let us not forfeit the glorious goodness of our humanity and the wonder of our very existence.

The Unitarian Universalists have grappled with this contradiction and disconnect since their merger. I am impressed and moved by the deep inquiry and the noble efforts of many who, early on asked, "Where is the Spirit? How do we bring it into the House of Worship?" This past month I read about the Charles Street Meeting House in Boston and was reminded that that was where my own family went to ask for support and solace during the Viet Nam War. I am surprised to see that much of what I learned about the intention of All Faiths Seminary was practiced there.

I can't help but believe that the six guiding principles of AFSI are very, very similar to the Guiding Testimonials of UU and the tenets of interfaith efforts more generally.

May I share them and then ask that we open up a discussion where you might share your own wisdom?

1. We affirm the truth in all faiths and religious paths.

2. We affirm our belief that seeking attunement to Spirit is the highest goal of conscious living.

3. We affirm an inclusive vision of "We."

4. We affirm the essential goodness of the human being.

5. We affirm that each person, indeed all life, is a part of the healing of the world.

6. We affirm the value of interfaith interactions as enriching our awareness of Spirit in the world.

Welcome Back

September 2014

Good morning and welcome back. Welcome back from a Summer of what was given, what was received and what was learned. Bring the lens of gratitude and look back as we prepare to move forward. Focus on the positive, holding that which has sustained you and brings you into the Fall with active hope.

To start with, it's been a summer of relative ease weather wise. The heat not too hot, the cool not to too cool. Not too much rain but no serious drought. Gratitude builds. A gratitude for a weather pattern that has moved us through a season often fraught with highs and lows.

The environmental conditions have not been so easy for others.

A huge dam in Canada breaks and floods thousands of acres (miles) with the toxic wastes of a tar sand mining industry unchecked. Two First Nation Reservations are lost, their five-year cry ignored.

The desertification of the western Bulge of Africa is an enemy, driving people out of their homelands. And the great glaciers slip away, bringing change we can't imagine, including methane holes in Siberia!

But stop and remember with gratitude the beauty of our world, this earth, this continent, and your own back yard. Remember the fullness of the harvests (though late), the clouds, the flowers, the vistas, the gentle rains.

The deer, bear, turkeys and birds have been more present and closer, insisting on sharing this world that is theirs as well as ours. We think we get it, but don't really know how to realize the shared and loved world with a one legged, two legged, four legged, winged and finned sentient family.

Gratitude in waves rolls in but is followed quickly by pain and confusion in the face of politically elusive realities. We "put our head in the sands" and say with a cynical abdication that "Whatever will be will be." This is hard for a grandmother who watches tomorrow's little people splashing in the surf, scrambling up a loved mountain, or reaching for little brother's hand as they walk through the woods. My four-year-old grandson Luc asked for "things that always are." Gratitude and love were all I could promise and that, only if we make room for it.

The summer has been full of conversations we dare to have in the face of the many uncharted waters. We describe a political Left which sounds like the old Right, the Right has created a new swing to the pendulum, and around the world, the extreme replaces the dream of democracy. The desperate hold on the white male privilege of colonialism dies hard with the inevitable changes in the balance of power. Rather than say "Yes" to a Black President, they will bring the entire thing down with no thought of the Seven Generations that are our responsibility.

But gratitude is the message this morning. Gratitude for the loved ones in our lives. Not always right, fair, or good, but they are there and are the backstop to our own being. Some are employed, some serving their country as teachers as well as service men and women. Some are full of hope and energy, others wondering what service means and why their PTSD can't be cured. The elders might provide a place of 'safe and steady' for a moment in the storm, even if we cannot provide a place of peace and freedom. The broken cry of Hallelujah is part of our gratitude. Life is a tough but ultimately loving teacher.

The summer has meant gatherings of multiple generations where too many block a conversation of substance, but where the dis-ease is averted by laughter that can be caught on the wind. Tears and gentle touches can bring truth and love to the reunion, memorial, birth, anniversary, wedding, divorce, job loss, family heartache. It is gratitude for the loving, love given, love received, love lost. A love that brings forth the best that we are.

All summer I found myself coming up into the love that surrounded me, even in the places of heartache, struggle, loss and anger. Love trumped all.

Three Stages of Life

October 2014

This summer I joined a Worship Sharing Group for Quakers 65 and older. We were given a question to consider and spoke out of the silence in response. I remember one man who spoke of the three stages of his life. As Quakers would say, he spoke to my condition.

He described the first third as his time of BECOMING, the second as the time of his DOING, and the third as his time of BEING.

Perhaps it was the intimate way in which he owned this process or the silence that followed that allowed us to hold the significance of his words. Whatever it was, it was a message that has resonated within me since. It has felt like a way of holding the complexity and awesomeness of a life. ...

BECOMING
Becoming was about coming into a self that lived in a family group that had expectations, assumptions, contradictions and responsibilities that you came to know while desperately trying to hold to your own unique being. Childhood is not an easy place. It can be a

cruel and unjust world that calls itself family and community. We can all remember our own struggle to know that we were who we were despite our place in the world. The social acquisition is nothing less than miraculous.

The universals of cultural survival are learned within the first 6 years of life, we are told. We learn to learn despite an educational system which focuses on teaching. We see the world despite the directions to look without seeing. We hear through the heart despite the focus on listening to the directives of both adults and peers. But we also, if lucky, swing from trees, play in the brook, run through a field, sit with a grandparent, hold a newborn sibling and know there are other teachers and other lessons to trust and be emboldened by.

I visualize that miraculous power of procreation that is the primal link for all sentient beings. I remember that awesome connection the moment I was handed my first baby. Her little fingers wrapped around my finger, and I was suddenly reassured that I belonged. Then there was the first time my infant son said "no" and then "habi", which we came to know as "help me." I felt the power of ones dependence, independence and then quickly the interdependence.

DOING

The doing of life is that time when the activities of the peopled world and all its roles are upon us: householder, spouse, parent, employee, citizen. We pull into the tribe the rights, the rules and the structures of our creation (institutions). Doing is being the actor on the stage of life, in the limelight or on the margins. There is a role to play and an audience that is judging you from its own place in the theater. They hold your attention and get your energy, be they your partner, your children, your boss, your party. Your dreams are achieved or not. We realize that a dream achieved is no longer a dream, but hard work and commitment.

Loving wavers; liking and disliking those one loves change the paradigm. We are holding on to what is ours and wanting to believe that we make our world happen. We protect, fix, fail, shore up, build and own, correct and control, rage, regret, impart and love. We are so right and so earnest....and then our idealism and energy wain. We believe that without us things would ...well, don't ask the question now that might come later. I hope for us all that it does come, for forgiveness and the solace of acceptance are the reward for making it this far.

BEING

Being is a time when the roles fall away like scaffolding around the real thing. The being is exposed and the process of becoming and doing is visible in the man or woman who stands before you. Things change again. Slowly we see that the roles, titles and labels fall away, and we are almost surprised to see that we are still here. Perhaps we are pushed into the role of elder, senior citizen or the dying by those who need the younger roles, but we are still here, and things seem to open up.

When asked by an essayist this summer what I could say about being one of the elders in my community, I heard myself say: "We are less identified with the "I"/mine" of the people world and can better see the "we" of the shared world, a natural world of extraordinary wonder. The connections are more apparent when you have seen the generations unfold, the world survive our selfish madness, and how the Earth Mother and Father Sky still hold us despite our folly. It is easier to let go of things, resentments, hurts, old ways, even children and loved ones. It is not the great sacrifice we feared it might be, but a release and freedom. One begins to respect, honor, and treasure the cycle of life that we are one with. Even death is embraced as it is. Life is not a fight but a sacred gift. Assumptions and expectations can fall away, they serve no purpose now, and reaching out to others is now an act of unencumbered generosity, love and reciprocity. Those that make it to Being become more static, not without purpose but as a lighthouse or a bridge for ourselves and others in a long-deferred service to the world and, indeed, to the Sacred web of Life."

The three stages are all part of the wholeness of a life. Lessons of all three stages constantly inform wherever you are. But the demarcation has helped me know, embrace, and love the gift of my time here. The river of life takes a lifetime to begin to appreciate. Life is not easy but, indeed, it is the sacred gift of NOW, wherever we are in the process. Perhaps it is possible to look back and reassure those who are in the midst of it all, that indeed, it is All Good.

The Original Instructions

Date unknown

In the tradition of the First Peoples, let me tell you a story, the medicine story of Hobbomokko and Cheepii as told by Manitonquat.

Hobbomokko ponders the inexplicable of creation and begins to question the possibility that all is perfect. This brings fear and a sense of disconnection to his friend, Cheepii. Cheepii tries to reassure Hobbomokko, but in doing so begins to neglect his vital role as steward and gardener. So things begin to go awry and Cheepii begins to share the doubt of Hobbomokko. Cheepii begins to defend himself against evil forces and dangers he had never noticed before. (I am reminded of the tests of both Jesus and Buddha, where they are tempted to forgo their knowing as integral beings.)

With neglect, the bonds that connect suffered, the garden withered, relationships unraveled, and people began to know Dis-Ease.

The people were alarmed and turned to Maushop, the elder. He explained that those who do not know or have forgotten the Original Instructions of creation are being pulled away from their center. He reminded the people of the three key instructions.

1. Notice how Creation works through observation of the Natural World.

2. Seek inside yourself, for the creator/creation also exists there.

3. The combination of the first two instructions coming together will create the world in which to live. All who have come before us and their observations and meditations will be shared, and in that ceremony of shared wisdom and gratitude, we will grow a world respectful of all.

The people remembered and returned to the world of [respect for] All My Relations.

Cheepii still clung to his fear but found few to follow him, and for 400 years all went well. But then a people wearing black, with a belief system grounded in fear, evil, sin and damnation landed on their shores and have ever since ridiculed and scorned the Original Instruction, ravaging the Mother and believing that Here is a place to use on the way to Somewhere Else. Cheepii's world of fear and deprivation had come to be.

A Hopi elder is quoted as saying of Mother Nature, "She is tired of the pesky mites who think they can run the show. She prepares to shake us off."

For all First People, it is through the Spirit of Creation that all things are related. The Original Instruction is found in that Law. All things follow the natural law. Humans are not above, beyond, or outside of that law. Within that law is the interconnectedness, balance, harmony, completeness, oneness of creation.

When we disconnect from the Original Instruction, we have severed the tie to our Spirit Guide and our Mother the Earth. Into that vacuum, we bring scripture, liturgy, idols and false gods in hopes of filling the void. We survive, progress and win, but only just. The time is running out.

The First Peoples from around the world are trying to call our attention to this. They are not a people lost to history, but alive. Though living in very "primitive" and often deprived conditions, they remember and are calling us to turn to the elders and, before it is too late, to ask once again for the Original Instruction which alone is essential to the balance and survival of our world. The teaching of the Original Instruction requires a wise and large-minded person, one who can see beyond fear and self. One who knows the difference between loving the flag and loving the land.

The Onandaga and people from twenty-seven Native Nations this summer paddled 207 miles with European brothers and sisters down the River of Life to bring the Original Treaty (between the Onandaga and the Dutch) to the UN.

There, Oren Lyons, the Faith Keeper of the Turtle Clan, was given a standing ovation when he said quietly from the dais:

> *The first time I came here for my clan, the second time for my tribe, the third time for my people, the fourth time for all Indigenous people from around the world. The fifth time I came to remind you that we MUST remember, not the seven generations before us, but the seven generations that come after us. This time I come to say we must remember All Our Relations. How do you teach seven billion people to remember the seven generations yet to come for whom we are accountable?*

Two months later, he stepped away with a broken spirit as he listened to the arrogance of power dash the promise to remember that "we do not inherit the Earth from our ancestors, but rather we borrow it from our children." The message that the earth is our home and not a resource for our exploitation fell on deaf ears at the Warsaw Climate Change Hearings.

I would encourage you to Google this man Oren Lyons and sit with the wisdom he shares. He is one of the few who can and will span the abyss that we have created between ourselves and the Mother that is our world.

People who have lived in hiding have now come forward out of the Amazon rainforest to tell us that they are sharing a dream. In that dream the Eagle (curiosity and disconnection) has flown too far outside of the spheres of safety for our world; and the great condor (ozone layer) must leave the world unprotected to go in search of the eagle and convince it to return and bring the wisdom of the world back. We (Two Legged) are, like the One Legged (the trees), rooted in the earth, reaching to the light but [bound to Earth as] our home and our source of creation. We must care for it if it is to care for us.

Others share a dream (planted by Frank Fools Crow) that not only were artifacts taken, but also much of the wisdom of the First People, and perhaps there are those among the whites who can help retrieve the Original Instruction before it is too late. Many who have stood in stony silence are reaching out for the first time to one another.

And finally, there is the remarkable synchronization that is coming all the way round to the wisdom of this Original Instruction from the realm of quantum physics. It is shared in the words of the astronauts upon their return from space and seen in the unravelling of systems and institutions which have met their end, be they banks, corporations, schools or religions. A paradigm shift is happening, and the First People may be the ones who still have an inclination towards what it might mean.

My personal experiences with the people of the First Nations have taught me the most profound lessons of my spiritual journey. Perhaps the most profound is that if you can "be as a hollow bone", the truth will come through you, not from you.

All My Relations (bowing)

The Jesus Story

December 24, 2013

In 2008, my daughter struggled with her desire to find the man with whom she would bear a child. The biological time clock was ticking. Love had flowered and fallen not once but a couple of times.

She had focused on setting the intention and asking deep questions of herself as to who and what she wanted. She had opened herself to a process that we rarely prepare for consciously.

That Christmas, we joined an annual living creche that gathers with singing and storytelling in an ancient barn. We had been to this event several times over the years and dear friends joined us. At the last minute, we heard that "Mary" couldn't make it and a friend asked Ami to fill in. "All you have to do is hold the baby," she said. So Ami reluctantly wrapped herself in the cloak and took the "baby" in her arms. She told me later that the process was strange and other worldly. She was not very articulate, but clearly moved by the experience.

The following April, we joined friends on an adventure in Guatemala. There, Ami encountered a wonderful old Pan of a man who...told her the story of a young Mayan woman who had sat on the ledge, high over the valley floor, for thousands of years, evidenced by the imprint of her hands and buttocks on the rocks still clearly visible today, waiting for just the right moment to leap into her life.

By August, Ami had found the man who shared her own dream, and before they knew it, they found themselves with child.

I am reminded of the line in the poem by O.R.Melling:

> *When you come to the edge of all that you know,*
> *you must believe one of two things: either there*
> *will be ground to stand on, or you will be given*
> *wings to fly.*

The story of Mary's immaculate conception, whether understood from a Catholic or Protestant point of view, like similar stories from other great prophetic voices, is a story we lean into as we reach...into the depths of ourselves and come forward with what feel like miracles. Perhaps Mary's story is the story of our yearning to give expression to our most realized selves.

Some will find this almost sacrilegious, but I think not.

Who, what is this child she brings forth? Is Jesus the expression of our deepest yearning? [Is Christ] the promise of the better self that lives just beyond the personality of this world of earthly calls? The promise that a world of justice is worth building? The promise that we can know ourselves as sacred beings, capable of great and simple unity, of shared caring that can bring us across the great abyss and back to connection?

We know that those better selves are required now perhaps like never before, as we face the re-writing of the script.

We know that the extreme fiscal inequality of Them and Us, the environmental risk of extinction, and the rupture within the community of the sacred have blocked light, love and life.

We know that we have come to the crossroad where we must center, surrender and let our decisions come from our better selves, daring to do what we have asked Jesus' life to represent for us. We must prepare to "jump," engage, respond, and open.

All the Jesus stories speak to that place in ourselves that affirms the very energy of which we are created and of which we are a part. We see it and are in awe, we join it, and it feels like there was no other way to respond. We cannot wait for a thousand years, and we cannot leave it up to a mythical story of one man's miraculous [influence]. We must jump. We must follow the example of the great prophetic traditions that have brought forward the same recurrent wisdom of the ages.

May I share two stories from 9/11 that bring this message home?

I was working at Camp La Guardia on 9/11 and eighty men, homeless and forgotten, crammed into the lunchroom and pleaded that we find busses to take them into NYC to help with the aftermath of the fall of the Twin Towers. Their testimonials were powerful, anguished cries to be useful and purposeful; an opportunity to have this gift of life earned and honored. I shared their tears of disappointment when they were refused.

The second story is that of the remarkable boatlift of over 500,000 people in nine hours from lower Manhattan on 9/11. I encourage you to watch the YouTube video. One man in New Jersey saw the buildings fall, turned to his wife and said, "I have to go." He took his luxury boat the "Amberjack" into the cloud of debris and devastation and began picking people up. Why? "Because if I don't, I'll always know I could have but I didn't."

A welder who was part of the effort is quoted as saying, "There's a hero inside all of us that will come out when needed." Others said of that day that it was about doing the right thing for the right reason, and it went without a hitch. Still others said, Though we thought everything fell apart, it was, in fact, the day that brought it all together, and there was a oneness that will never be forgotten.

We have all known that better self, that Jesus consciousness, that "hero." We know what Jesus would have done. We know the simple and profound love that his story represents; it is our story, too.

For me, Christmas is a time of rejuvenation and renewal, and it reminds me that we are born again and again into the possibility of our better selves, fuller selves, heroes of love with the promise of the Jesus within of us. We are all born of wonder under a star of light, gifted with the gift of everlasting life.

Namaste

Gaia: Mothers' Day

May 2014

Mother Earth, Earth Mother, Gaia, Tara, Terra, Pachamama, the Great Mother, Mother, Mama, Mom: every origin story places her front and center. We are born into being. Mother bears us, suckles us, nurtures us. We are of her being, but free to be ourselves. Life gives life.

The essential fact of this miracle is all too often obfuscated behind the arrogance of ego and twisted projections. What if we look more carefully, what if we ask ourselves what Mother means? Where is she in our lives? What have we brought with us from all that she provided for us?

What would the world look like if it was Matriarchal rather than Patriarchal? What was the world that existed before the rise of Christianity? Where is Mary in the story of Jesus? What happens to Christianity when Mary comes forward? Why has Mary been relegated to almost no role at all in the Protestant religions, yet in Latin cultures is the focal point of faith?

"Mother Mary comes to me, speaking words of wisdom, let it be....."

The remarkable lyrics of Paul McCartney's song about his calling out to his own dead mother in despair, and her answer "let it be," took the world by storm. Mother's steadying influence is crucial to our equilibrium. She is there in the lullaby you sing to your own child, the sacrifice you make, the instinctual right that you know, the anguish in the cry against injustice and the wrenching heartache of love beyond reason. She is there beyond the grave. She IS; without her we don't exist.

I have intentionally moved back and forth between the Great Mother, Mary the mother of Christianity, and our mortal mothers. Mom is mortal and full of fault and guilt, and her sacrifice is invisible to her as well as to us. She gives because she cannot not, she loves because there is no other way forward, she moves beyond tired into what looks like an abdication of self and power, but don't be fooled....

Mother by definition is the origin of beginning. The process of carrying, delivering and caring for a child is what brings us into the social whole that we know. The long period of gestation and dependence of the human child is like no other. It is that relationship that gives rise to our social groupings and our cultural mores. That need to be carried, fed, held, allows for a bonding between mother and child that is unlike any other species.

Pause and consider the Great Earth Mother. Consider our relationship to her. Consider the exploitation, ravaging, disregard, oblivious self-interest, and ask if or for how long will this relationship be tolerated? When will she say, "Enough is enough"? When will she shake us off?

Great Mother Earth, giver of all life,

Remember that in our time here, we have become the indulged and selfish ones who are reminded of the great sacrifice required only when we, too, are called into the maternal knowing of parenting.

May we learn again what you are always showing us, but we have become too disconnected to see, hear, know.

We exist because of the intricate miracle of the life-giving qualities of your body, our body, a Body that you alone can provide.

Forgive us our arrogant belief that we can do it without you. Forgive us our forgetfulness.

Thank you for the carpet of green, the burst of yellow in the fields, woods and gardens, the soft dark healing nights, the colors of the rising and setting sun, the cleansing rains, the rushing rivers, the blue skies and all the bounty that is our sustenance and your life-giving gift.

Mothers of always and forever, we remember with deep gratitude the love, the sacrifice, and the everlasting promise of today. May we remember the tomorrows of our children and our children's children.

We have forgotten who we are.
We have alienated ourselves from the unfolding of the cosmos.
We have become estranged from the movements of the earth.
We have turned our backs on the cycles of life
We have forgotten who we are.

We have sought only our own security.
We have exploited simply for our own ends.
We have distorted our knowledge.
We have abused our power.
We have forgotten who we are.

Now the land is barren
And the waters are poisoned
And the air is polluted.
We have forgotten who we are.

Now the forests are dying
And the creatures are disappearing
And the humans are despairing.
We have forgotten who we are.

We ask forgiveness.
We ask for the gift of remembering.
We ask for the strength to change.
We ask that we remember that the earth is our
Mother.

Giving and Receiving at Christmas

December 2012

The swing between gift giving and receiving moves uncomfortably in this holiday season.

We are exposed and vulnerable. Generosity of spirit and gratitude toward ourselves and each other wane all too quickly.

Expectation trumps all. Competition challenges our insecurities about worth and value. The Christmas message is lost in the scramble to meet the "I want."

"The Gift of the Magi" was not on the front table in any of the bookstores I visited this week.

My children tolerated the handmade gifts even less than we did as children. What we wanted and what we got quickly (before we were six or seven or eight) determined our social definition of the success of Christmas.

But there were places there for lessons that meant more than we realized.

I remember today the carved pig that still is the cutting board in my brother's home, and the iron fire poker made by my son that still is at my fireplace.

I learned compassion and remorse when I sulked because I didn't get the bathrobe I wanted, and I felt my mother suffer my disappointment more than I did.

My son says the most important Christmas lesson for him was listening to his older sister blaming me for not giving her a Christmas like her friends got. His heart broke for me, and he struggles to this day to forgive his sister such selfishness.

The singular memory of my six siblings is the Christmas when there were no gifts from our father under the tree but a canoe in the barn and the vague promise of finding a place in the spring to paddle it. Our minds soared and dreamed, and then there was a tiny cabin in all its simple rustic beauty, and a lovely lakefront that we, to this day, have held on to as the family [configuration alters and grows.]

I carried on the tradition of stockings filled with tools of practicality: the new toothbrush, a vegetable peeler, a book of stamps, a tangerine, a potholder, a favorite candy bar, a new kind of soap, vitamins, etc. When the kids left home, they enquired as to how the stocking would arrive. They didn't want that to be replaced or forgotten because that was what they remembered most.

May I ask you to remember the rituals of this holiday, the food, the music, the decorations, the unfolding of the day, and pick out from the tumble of excess and stuff what rings true? What can you smell, see, feel? Even in the pain, look for the lesson, the opening or closing of your heart.

What has continued to inform your life, your spirit, your hope?
Where was the giving as much cherished as the receiving?
What was that gift wrapped in?
How was it given and received? I will guess with LOVE.

As the Christmas Season falls down upon us, may we remember and retell the stories of what we cherished, what we learned, what we truly gave and what we truly received on this day that is so full of joy and heartache, excess and longing, connection and isolation.

Give the gift that connects. Give Love and take Joy.

I salute you! There is nothing I can give you which you have not; but there is much, that, while I cannot give, you can take.

No heaven can come to us unless our hearts find rest in it today. **Take Heaven.**

No peace lies in the future which is not hidden in this present instant. **Take Peace.**

The gloom of the world is but a shadow; behind it, yet, within our reach, is joy. **Take Joy.**

And so . . . I greet you, with the prayer that for you, now and forever, the day breaks and the shadows flee away.

Fra Giovanni (we think)

Amazing Grace

January 2013

Grace is what I believe in and reach for. It guides my practice and reveals my faith. It comforts and heals me, and in it I find forgiveness and love. In my exploration of Grace for today, I have found much written, but in the end, I bring it down to simple sentences that I share with you today. I encourage you to consider your own understanding of this gift that is always there for us.

Grace is kindness.
Grace is the lifting of spirit.
Grace is participation in the whole, beyond self.
Grace is the ability to rise above the mental forces of fear and limitation, thus attaining the power to heal and be healed.
Grace isn't a little prayer before a meal but a way of life.
Grace is found in hospitality, not in service, healing not in fixing, faith not in religion.
Grace never ignores the awful truth of hurt, sickness, cruelty and all our depravity, but sees it, then, without judgement.
Grace emanates from within and radiates outward.

Grace reflects the best.
Grace is there always and everywhere.
Grace is perception with love.
Grace is the lubricant for a loving and peaceful life.

I asked a half a dozen people to share with me their understanding of Grace. All hesitated, quieted, and moved into a different place before answering. Their bodies shifted, four literally sighed. Their voices softened and their faces relaxed. All journeyed down into the depth and breadth of the word.

Some came from a Christian understanding: Grace is unmerited mercy, salvation, Divine guidance, the presence of God.

Others described Grace in adjectives: To be receptive, graceful, respectful, gracious, fully present, not boastful, flowing, humble, responsive, discerning, enlightened, kind, loving, forgiving.

All commented on the great value of considering Grace. Several expressed gratitude for the shift they experienced in themselves in the very consideration of Grace. One felt healed and uplifted, one forgiving of themselves and another, and still a third felt a softening and release after a relatively brief conversation.

Grace is the "balm of Gilead that heals the sin-sick soul." It is the salve of forgiveness with compassion. Judgement is absent.

How many of us have said, "There, but for the grace of God, go I," feeling a gratitude while at the same time a heartache for the other who must travel that road. God's grace has nothing to do with wrath, revenge, or punishment. Grace is a love that is unconditional, holds, comforts, and is present and revealed. Grace makes whole that which feels separate. Amen.

Sermon on Light

March 2013

I was only about nine or ten and loved going on "house calls" with my father, who was a family doctor.

Story # 1.

On one cold Sunday afternoon, I sat for a long time in the car, waiting for my father to come from the large, stately house with only one small light in the window. When he did, it was with a vigorous and almost buoyant stride. I remember wondering what he had found in there.

He looked at me with surprise and said, "Oh dear, I had forgotten you were here." He then proceeded to tell me the story of his house call. May Jacobs, an elderly, wise and worldly woman, was sitting in the darkening afternoon light when my father arrived.

"She asked me to shed some light on her dying. I turned on the light. We both laughed and laughed until tears filled her eyes, and she said, "It is really that simple. I just need to dare turn on the light."

I never forgot that afternoon. I remember my father saying that the dying were the only ones who dared to see the truth. I remember, too, the bounce in his step and the warmth in the car as soon as he got in. I knew I wanted his perspective.

Here after fifty years, I find myself asking: So what is "Light"? Clarity, warmth, being seen, connection, a place of trust, being loved, loving, being understood, comforted, grounded, without fear. Or perhaps we could call it: Spark, Holy Spirit, source of Life, Grace, or God's holy light.

Call it what you will, light is born of the dark. The light is given its depth, perspective and vibrance by the dark.

Story #2   Mandala at Healing Circle

Coming to the Light implies choice, clarity and trust. But we often **choose** the darkness for fear of what the light may reveal. We block the eyes, ears and voice of the heart in fear of not finding what we think we want or can control. We confuse our perceptions as truth and don't see them as the projections that block what IS.

Birth and death are two of the greatest teachers. There we can be forced to get out of the way of the light. Our own shadow disappears, and we see clearly and face to face.

Story #3 Stepping away from self

We step away from ourselves to welcome another at the time of birth, and at the time of combat. Remember giving birth or experiencing a life-threatening moment. Who steps forward, and what are their priorities, perspectives?

What brings us to the light? Is it our perspective? Our worldview? Our receptivity? Our ability to accept?

Or must we surrender our ego-built world, the one where we are the center fold, or are outside looking in at a dream we think we created   We must believe in a self beyond ego and its institutions. We must believe that we are a thread in the tapestry of life. It dips and weaves throughout our journey here and is unique; but alone, it creates little.

So then, who holds the light for us? Who or what holds the door to this warmth, courage and clarity?

Loved ones, trusted ones, music, art, discovery from books, teachers, the natural world---all can all hold open the door, but only we can pass through it. The moment when we know that all is right with the world despite our protestations, we can, with a leap of faith, call upon an [inner] Self of love and light that will come forward and lead the way. (I choose not to use the word God here only because, for many, God is not within.)

A friend who was dying asked, "What would call you to the other side?" Without much thought I said, "If I heard my father whistle." He smiled and said, "Yes, of course, that's what I am waiting for."

Darkness implies depression, despair, "evil" and "sin", yet we know that we are often the one who casts the shadow, and that darkness often comforts and quiets a restless mind. It is often in the dark that we discover the insights of enlightenment and the quiet safety that comes as we surrender each night to sleep.

Out of the dark comes the light. In the dark, a tiny spark can be seen by many. The light becomes the beacon of promised connection. The lighthouse provides a centering point, a marker or a harbor in a heartless world. Light brings us into proximity WITH.

The darkness can also sever the sense of connection so that we are convinced that we are alone, adrift. The smoke and mirrors of our projections and self-pictures elude and distort. The illusory world that we call real takes hold, and we are lost in the dreams and daydreams of ego. Darkness descends.

When we turn on the light, we awake and are found, seen, even loved. The really transformative moments in our lives can put us back on our path. As we look into the harsh light of truth, we see that light restores and realigns us. We can even look into the face of death. The darkness is put in perspective, knowing becomes intuitive, and the path becomes clear. Our smallness is lost to the greatness of who we are and of all that we are an integral part of.

We are integrated into the spirit of creation, held in the circle of Mother Earth, Father Sky and the Spirits of the four directions. Light and dark are balanced in the dance of our existence. Light and dark, right and wrong, good and evil, black and white are but the swing of a never-ending pendulum that ego, in its separation from Source, has judged and dichotomized, leaving us alone in the dark. Dare to turn on the light and you'll see the dark that gives the vibrancy of contrast, wonder and integration to wholeness.

The Father who holds the light, the vibrancy of the Mandala, and the gift of trusting those that hold the door can be found in all of our stories. May you consider their place in yours. Turn on the light.

Sacred Seven

March 2014

There is, I think, for all of us a bit of mystery in the number seven. All cultures reflect its power as we look at the world inside and out.

There are the Sacred Seven of the four directions (north, east south and west), the earth mother, father sky and the Creator of our opening this morning.

There are seven parts of the body internal and external: two arms, two legs, body, thorax and head. There are the seven openings of the head: two eyes, two ears, two nostrils and the mouth. The seven organs of life (the brain, heart, liver, kidneys, lungs, stomach), and the seven internal systems (respiratory, circulatory, alimentary, excretion, reproductive, sensory and reactive) all provide functions essential to life.

Now remember the 7 planets, 7 oceans, 7 continents, 7 notes in our scale, 7 colors in a prism, 7 wonders of the world, and the special status of the seventh son of a seventh son.

We carry that seven with us and find it is a theme used again and again, be it a sacred or secular context.

Consider the theme of seven in dozens of novels and movies from every culture. Think of them: James Bond 007, Seven Years in Tibet, Seven Brides for Seven Brothers, The Seven Faces of Dr Lao, Seven Pounds, The Seventh Seal, Seven Seconds.

No wonder seven has come to pervade the great religions. All religions find 7 to be fundamental. Consider the 7 rays of the Hindu sun and 7 chakras; the 7 faces of Buddha; the 7 candles in the Menorah, the 7 feasts of purification and 7 pillars of Jewish wisdom; in Islam, the 7 heavens, hells, earths, and seas, and the 7 doors to paradise. Don't forget the 600+ references to 7 in the Bible: 7 days of creation, 7 sacraments, 7 virtues, 7 sins, 7 joys, 7 sorrows and 7th seal of God. On the seventh day, God rested and called the world whole and holy.

Masons who have ancient origins and a very contemporary presence know the Letter G for God is the 7th letter in the alphabet. As Masons and builders, the number 7 pervades their language of knowing. Remember Dan Brown's "The Lost Symbol."

On the Wiccan path, where numerology and astrology are so significant, the number 7 represents the lunar energy of the moon, femininity, and workings related to intuition and wisdom consciousness.

And Theosophists explain the world in seven principles, a synthesis of Eastern and Western ideas that are identified with all new age thinking.

They are:

1. Sharia is the physical body,
2. Linga Sharira the astral body,
3. Prana the vital source,
4. Kamarupa the body of desire,
5. Manas the higher Ego and ordinary mind,
6. Buddhi the spiritual soul, the vehicle of the pure universal spirit,
7. Atma the Spirit or Self.

And finally, consider the seven principles of UU, a path to living a whole and useful life.

1. The inherent worth and dignity of every person,
2. Justice, equity and compassion in human relations,
3. Acceptance of one another and encouragement to spiritual growth in our congregations,
4. A free and responsible search for truth and meaning,

5. The right of conscience and the use of the democratic process within our congregation and in society at large,
6. The goal of world community with peace, liberty and justice for all,
7. Respect for the interdependent web of all existence of which we are a part.

So what in the end do we have to conclude but that in the natural order of things, there is a gathering of seven that brings forth the whole. A completion: fulfilled, satisfied in entirety, perfection, the cycle completed, enough.

I cannot lay this powerful symbol down without mentioning a wonderful and insightful reworking of the theme of seven in Mahatma Gandhi's list of *The Seven Destructive Blunders of the World* that are the cause of violence.

1. Wealth without work
2. Pleasure without conscience
3. Knowledge without character
4. Commerce without morality
5. Science without humanity
6. Religion without sacrifice
7. Politics without principle

May we carry seven with us over the next seven days and remember to bring to this 7th day a moment of awe and gratitude for all that has come our way and all that we have been protected from. And may we remember that a life worth living is a life of work, conscience, character, morality, humanity, sacrifice and principle.

Pearl Harbor Day and Forgiveness

December 2013

I said last summer I would like to think about Forgiveness for the December Fellowship. On November 24th, Judi said; "Your next service will be on Pearl Harbor and Forgiveness." I was startled and felt the power of the two ideas boomerang through my heart and mind. I had spent a lifetime trying to avoid Pearl Harbor and those horrific consequences.

December 2, 1945 is my birthday, the Tule Lake Japanese War Relocation Camp my birthplace. World War II was a heartache that brought me into the world under the most unreal of circumstances with contradictions that were never processed, reconciled or forgiven.

And today I am called to address the subject from a place of objective reflection and responsive reconciliation. Once again, this strange invitation to share sacred stories with you brings me forward.

You all know that the "day of infamy" was Dec.7, 1941, when six Japanese aircraft carriers provided 353 bombers, torpedo planes and Zero fighters to attack a sleepy and hung-over American fleet of war ships waiting for action. Within an hour, war was declared. The Pacific War raged for the next six horrific years.

Within hours of the attack, reeling from the terrible loss of 1500 killed on the ships and the loss of our own American fighter jets brought down by friendly fire, people of any Japanese ancestry on the west coast were rounded up and sent to a barb-wired field called Sands Detention Camp. It was the first of ten such concentration camps. Most Japanese Americans had immigrated to the US between 1890 and 1915, and America had been their home for generations. But fear drove us.

On February 19, 1942, Roosevelt signed Executive Order 9066, which forced all Japanese-Americans, regardless of loyalty or citizenship, to evacuate the West Coast. Ten internment camps were established, in California, Idaho, Utah, Arizona, Wyoming, Colorado and Arkansas, eventually holding 120,000 persons.

Not until 1952 were Japanese American immigrants allowed to become naturalized US citizens. Not until last month was Executive Order 9066 removed from the books.

Tule Lake Relocation (Concentration) Camp in northern California was the camp were any Japanese Americans who refused to sign the Loyalty Oath were held until 1946, a year after the war was over on September 2, 1945. They feared the signing because of the consequences to family and friends still living in Japan.

On August 6, 1945, the United States dropped the first atomic bomb on Hiroshima and on August 9, 1945, the United States dropped a hydrogen bomb on Nagasaki. Within the first two to four months of the bombings, the acute effects killed 90,000–166,000 people in Hiroshima and 60,000–80,000 in Nagasaki, with roughly half of the deaths in each city occurring on the first day. During the following months, large numbers died from the effect of burns, radiation sickness, and other injuries compounded by illness. In both cities, most of the dead were civilians.

My father, a conscientious objector to war, was a doctor and my mother an English teacher, at first one and then a second camp. They were at Tule Lake at the time of the bombing.

My mother tells me that the woman who was helping her with her children came tell her that she must take the day off. When my mother asked why, infamy beyond Infamy was uttered in a whispered cry: her entire family had lived in Hiroshima.

The fear of genocide in the camps, which happening in Europe, had been realized in Japan on a scale and in a way that could not be spoken. Not by anyone. Not even today except in a whisper. No other people have used The Bomb not once but twice within a week.

My pregnant mother lost a baby that August but nevertheless gave birth to twins on December 2. (Originally, she had been pregnant with triplets!) Our first six months were a part of WRA camp life as it slowly rolled to a close and the horror of all that had unfolded became clear.

Within the Japanese-American community, there was never an act of disloyalty or espionage found. The most decorated unit in the entire US Army was the 442 Regiment composed of all Japanese Americans. The war was ostensibly over when still we dropped the bombs to make a point heard and felt around the world.

The story of the war was subdued as we grew up. Our friends talked of the brilliant heroism of Americans while quietly my parents displayed lovely gifts of Japanese art and musical instruments. Visiting guests regarded these things with quiet respect, but I don't remember any explanation forth coming from them or my parents as to where they came from. I never spoke to anyone who had any personal knowledge of the camps.

It became a family secret which couldn't be integrated socially. Both my parents' life work focused on the horrific fallout on both body and soul of that tragic moment, but little specific conversation could bridge the abyss to what they had experienced. In the words of Dave Dellinger, when asked why he remained an activist throughout his life, he said; "It was the exposure to the victims...."

Fast-forward 65 years. I am at a party and a Jewish friend is talking to an elderly Japanese American. She suddenly waves at me across the room and insists that I come now. The man takes my hands in his, they are trembling, his eyes fill with tears. He asks; "Is it true? were you born in a camp in California?" I say "yes" and feel my own eyes fill with tears and my hands tremble in his. "Tule Lake?" I can't speak but nod my head. He asks me to come and see him so we might speak of what is not spoken of.

Two weeks later, I visit the house he is preparing to sell. He serves me coffee and ice cream, tells me of his years as a young man struggling with all that is unravelling, and then shows me around the house. At the top of the stairs, he walks down the hall, stands in front of a beautiful jade mosaic, speaks softly to it, lifts it off the wall, brings it to me and says, "For you." I pause and look deep into his eyes. He says, "We are re-writing those days of infamy." I say "Re-membering." He says, *I've been looking for someone to help me lay all that to rest. Who would have thought it was an all-American white girl, born in that place.*

This past Monday, on December 2nd, my birthday, I received a lovely calendar from this same man, identifying himself as the former American President of Japanese Air Lines.

The serendipity of all this has spun out in all directions. Last week friends from the Bruderhoff just happened to bring me a book on Pearl Harbor and Manzanar, the first WRA camp. They tell me that they have just visited Pearl Harbor. They go on to tell me about a man named Glenn Paige who had been a part of the travesty of the Atomic Bomb, who woke up one morning in 1990, realized that he owed the rest of his life to help turn the world away from war, and is developing a social order of "non-killing."

And finally, in one of the interviews that came out of the Pearl Harbor Gathering of Reconciliation in 1991, I read that one of the Japanese bomber pilots, Zenji Abe, and Major Sargent Richard, on one of the ships that were bombed, forgave one another. Richards said, "It's been 60 years now. When you stop and think about it, the Japanese soldiers were doing their job and we were doing ours. It just happened that our jobs were to kill each other." Every two months, Zenji Abe paid for two roses that Richards placed at the Arizona Memorial and played taps as a tribute to all who died. They did this 140 times before Richard's death in 2004.

Forgiveness is the only way forward. Forgiveness is the promise of unconditional love. Forgiveness lives on the other side of Fear.

May we practice a fearless life.

Holding the Center

April 2014

Last week we spoke of finding Home, finding the center where there is a place you can let yourself be known and trust that others want to know you. A place where you share a vibration with all that is, and know you are connected.

How, when, where can we find that place?

Carlos Castaneda is said to have been told by Don Juan, the Yaqui shaman, "Examine your life for the monumental moments, the moments of knowing through feeling your human condition." He advised that we examine our teachers, all our teachers (people, places, experiences), and reflect on the lessons learned. He encouraged us to consider ourselves the creator of our own lives.

I encourage us all to try it. My experience in doing this? What a journey! what a labyrinth! What gratitude!

I discovered that the way I share my world is the way I share myself. My compassion for others was a measure of the compassion I showed myself. It was my compassion that opened doors and my heart. Moments of humiliation were where I discovered humility.

In short, where you put your attention, that is where you will find your life.

Hindsight has helped me see the truth of this insight. I have watched loved ones who have sustained a life of open optimism and hope, then when confronted with obstacles to that good will, succumbed too rapidly.

I have watched those who saw the world as a place of mean heartache and lived a life in which they bristled with regret and pity, and then, when stricken with disease, remembered the gift of life and embraced it with both arms, living well beyond the prognosis with deep love and gratitude.

I have no answers here but dare to testify to a life open to joy, light, and love. Not in the packaged conventional sense of the word, but with spontaneity and good heart, at least much of the time.

I have been accused of being a Pollyanna and an innocent. Both words might fit, but more accurately, I choose to put my attention on that which might encourage me and draw me beyond my mistakes, failures and insecurities.

To fail is to pause and consider the center. First you see yourself, you remember that you have failed before, you recognize that you will fail again, and you forgive yourself and embrace the humility in that knowing. I have heard it said, "Not until you are down, do you look up."

Life is what we choose.

The Lakota say you must choose life or you, by default, choose death. This lesson came to me as a young woman during the Viet Nam War, and it tore me apart. So many young men I knew had been drafted. Those who refused to fight and to kill paid dearly as conscientious objectors, but not with their lives. Meanwhile, those young people on the Rosebud Reservation who seemed to die with no explanation, were quietly said to have chosen death. (Bad Hand Family story).

The gift of life is given, the way we live it is up to us.

Mother Theresa is said to have responded to a nun who complained of listening for God's response for some thirty years to no avail, "Only thirty years?" Her life was not dependent on God's directive but on her own practice.

The Buddha is said to have responded to a student who wanted the answer to life: "Each morning we are born again, what we do today is up to us."

And William Least Heat Moon, a Native American, quotes his father, saying:

> *It is a contention of my father's, believing as he does that anyone who misses the journey misses about all he's going to get, that people become what they pay attention to. Our observations and our curiosity, they make and remake us.*

Our happiness is far more within our grasp than we let ourselves know. Our frustration and fear are the ego getting in the way of the wonder and miracle of what we might welcome if we held that need to control and judge at bay.

A 93-year-old friend said to me this week, "If I can remember that I am here to be cared for and that is my role, everything is lovely. When I don't, I can't appreciate how well we all work together." Marian is suffering from dementia; perhaps we all need a little of that to find the life given.

The Paradoxical Commandments
by Dr. Kent M. Keith

People are illogical, unreasonable, and self-centered.
Love them anyway.

If you do good, people will accuse you of selfish ulterior motives.
Do good anyway.

If you are successful, you will win false friends and true enemies.
Succeed anyway.

The good you do today will be forgotten tomorrow.
Do good anyway.

Honesty and frankness make you vulnerable.
Be honest and frank anyway.

The biggest men and women with the biggest ideas can be shot down by the smallest men and women with the smallest minds.
Think big anyway.

People favor underdogs but follow only top dogs.
Fight for a few underdogs anyway.

What you spend years building may be destroyed
overnight.
Build anyway.

People really need help but may attack you if you
do help them.
Help people anyway.

Give the world the best you have and you'll get
kicked in the teeth.
Give the world the best you have anyway.

Re-Membering

October 14, 2012

Re-membering the Source of all life is daunting, so I ask you just to consider your hand. See it, feel it, know what it does for you, what you can do with it. It is not manufactured but created. Created by that inexplicable Source.

Re-member the power of our Earth Mother. Consider the majesty of the seas, rivers, mountains, soil beds, seeds, flora and fauna. Consider and pause. Look at the shaft of wheat in your hand and consider the relationship between the hand and seed. Together, they are the manna of life, the bread of life.

Re-member the Ancestors who have brought us forward through the lives of hunters and gatherers, primitive farmers and on into the agricultural revolution. Consider their relationship to the world they knew. "Beauty before them, beside them, beauty behind them, beauty above them and beauty below them." Whatever we do to the web, we do to ourselves, and ALL are related.

I remember two children on the Navaho Reservation, where I lived for a summer in a village called Kayenta, home of the Owl. These two children stayed with me because their grandmother already had too many in her hogan. When I invited them to draw a picture, they drew trees with root systems almost as ornate as the branches. Child psychologist Jonathon Coles found this response among many indigenous people. These children understood the depths of their roots, and they knew the gifts of the world with which they were so intricately connected.

Remember your own ancestors, your parents, grandparents, even great grandparents. Remember their hands holding that manna. Consider their labors of love and toil in the struggle to survive and bring you forward. The Lakota say a life is fourteen generations, seven before you and seven beyond you. What do you carry with you from forebears? What will you pass on?

Remember the Norwegian immigrants in their sod homes on the verge of madness in their isolation from the mid-1800s to the early 1900s, in what we call today "America's Bread Basket."

Remember the Irish in waves escaping the great potato famine or those seeking not only nourishment of the body but also of the spirit who came in search of religious freedom and new frontiers.

And remember, today, those who till the soil, seed the field, harvest the abundance that we call by brand names and look for in boxes. Consider the world they know. Beauty before them, beside them....? Do we recognize the labor they do to sustain and nourish us? Is our gratitude evident?

Remember the child of the farmworker today who places the ritual object (bowl, basket, gourd, candle) at the family alter in each of the shanties they squat in as they follow the crops.

Remember the seed swollen with life, cracking the hull, sprouting, reaching up to the warmth of the sun and down to the water and nutrients in the soil. Creation of the perfect from the Perfect in a world that is one.

Now, can we remember what we have harvested this year? Consider what you feel deeply grateful for. Consider what it was you planted---an idea, an attitude, an intention, a seed.

What seed did you plant? What did someone else plant for you? What flowered, bore fruit, gratified you, brought you forward and connected you to the Source?

What intention built a soil able to nurture the outcome? Have you been able to share it in a way that nurtures others?

What didn't work? Why? Where was your attention, what was your level of preparedness, understanding, commitment?

What have you reaped?

Remembering the fruits of our labor is often forgotten, overlooked. We don't see our survival directly connected to our work. The supermarket is around the corner.

I ask you to consider what is growing in your life? Where did it come from? Who planted it? Is it feeding you, nurturing you, sustaining you? Does it come from the Source, from Perfection?

From which fruits that you have harvested do you want to save the seed?

Stop and think again. In the bright moon light of the Fall Equinox, as we move into the increasing darkness,

126

shrouded in a change that we do not fully comprehend, let us together remember "Life Ever After" and "World without End." Pause and consider the harmony, abundance and love that is and always has been our most awe-full and wonder-filled harvest, the Manna that we must never take for granted. Remember our connection, our Source, and our Perfection. We are one Creation. What we do to one, we do to all.

Lean on Me: Fathers' Day

June 2014

Fathers!!!

In my own story, Father was the most important of connections. Father defined the world. Father trusted the gift of life. He promised me that I could trust, trust the process even when I felt off kilter, offline or simply off. He provided the light house not only for me but for many. He promised that to "expect a miracle" would keep me awake and alert to the magnificence of our time here. He promised comfort when fear and self- doubt took hold.

A friend told me recently of a dying man recalling the father he needed now.

> *I remember as just a small boy, my father reprimanded me for misbehaving at the dinner table and then sent me to my room alone on the un-lit third floor of the house. After a bit he came into the room and found me frightened and on my knees praying in the dark. He kneeled down beside me, we recited the 23rd Psalm, he helped me into bed, tucked me in, kissed me good night*

and I was quiet and safe in the dark. I need him
now.

He is lucky to have that memory of guidance and comfort. Father, for too many, is a figment of imagination, be it the unknown biological father, the abstract father promising that "we'll get together soon" (remember Harry Chapin's *Cats in the Cradle*), or the Father in Heaven, up there somewhere.

Father, if you are lucky enough to have one in your life, knows the sanctity of his role. He leads, restores, prepares, provides, protects, comforts and holds a place of safety even as he struggles, worries, strives, loses and tries again.

Philip Booth in his poem, "First Lesson," teaches his daughter to swim. The first lesson is to float ie, to trust. Can you remember that first moment when you realized that the water was holding you and your dad who brought you to that place had stepped aside?

This past week an 85-year-old woman told me about her life as a shepherdess. She told me that the staff she carried served the function of marking the place of safety, food and community for the lost sheep. She described how the sheep would look for that crook of the tall staff and follow it home. She explained that the rod was carried but never used except to point the way. As she spoke, I could not help but remember the 23rd Psalm: "Thy rod and thy staff, they comfort me."

I think of the Father Sky who holds the vast unknown, unknowable. Every culture has its Sky Father, Father Sky, Zeus, Jupiter, Sky God that compliments Mother Earth. We only begin to understand the remark- able wisdom of the composite mythologies created from the mapping of the stars. It is no wonder that the western religions took hold of that realm to create its own monotheism.

But I would suggest that the great tragedy is that the projection of God into the Heavens created a great schism between earth and sky, female and male, intuition and intellect, right and wrong, and the general polarization of our understanding. The sacrifice of integration, wholeness, oneness has been great and grievous, too great.

The Judeo-Christian world split and polarized the sacred union of creation by creating a patriarchy that did a disservice to both men and women. Many writers have described how this happened.

I am reassured and gratified by the deep connection that I have witnessed between my son and my sons-in-law and their young boys. As women have gone into the work force, there has developed an irrefutable need for men to come into the home in ways unthinkable only a generation ago.

We must bring father back into our lives as the one who we can lean on, not because he is all knowing but because he loves us; not because he holds the power, but because he cares; not because we fear him, but because we trust him; not because he is in heaven, but because he is us and we are him.

In the celebration of union and creation, may we be strengthened, nurtured, comforted, loved and made whole, and reconnected to that from which we can be separated only by our own projections and confusion.

May we lean into the protection of our fathers, look for the rod and the staff that can comfort us, trust the process that they brought us to, honor their courage and sacrifice, and feel gratitude for the light house they represent for us, their precious children, even as we flail about out there on the waves of the open sea. Amen

The 23rd Psalm

*The Lord is my shepherd; I shall not want. He maketh
me to lie down in green pastures: he leadeth me beside
the still waters. He restoreth my soul: he leadeth me in
the paths of righteousness for his name's sake. Yea,
though I walk through the valley of the shadow of death,
I will fear no evil, for thou art with me; thy rod and thy
staff they comfort me. Thou preparest a table before me
in the presence of mine enemies: thou anointest my head
with oil; my cup runneth over. Surely goodness and
mercy will follow me all the days of my life: and I will
dwell in the house of the Lord forever.*

I Would Be True

I would be true, for there are those who trust me;
I would be pure, for there are those who care;
I would be strong, for there is much to suffer;
I would be brave, for there is much to dare;
I would be brave, for there is much to dare.

I would be friend of all—the foe, the friendless;
I would be giving, and forget the gift;
I would be humble, for I know my weakness;

I would look up, and laugh and love and lift.
I would look up, and laugh and love and lift.

Who is so low that I am not his brother?
Who is so high that I've no path to him?
Who is so poor, that I may not feel his hunger?
Who is so rich I may not pity him?
Who is so rich I may not pity him?

Who is so hurt I may not know his heartache?
Who sings for joy my heart may never share?
Who in God's heaven has passed beyond my vision?
Who to Hell's depths where I may never fare?
Who to Hell's depths where I may never fare?

May none, then, call on me for understanding,
May none, then, turn to me for help in pain,
And drain alone his bitter cup of sorrow,
Or find he knocks upon my heart in vain.
Or find he knocks upon my heart in vain.

By Howard Arnold Walter, 1917

EASTER: Rise Again

April 2014

On this long-awaited day this particular year, after a winter that held on for so long, the symbolism of Easter, Passover, Spring, Rebirth, the return to the Good Heart has a powerful message for us.

I have looked back at this annual occasion in my own life and am reminded that perhaps the most profound spiritual/religious experience I ever had was the Yaqui Easter Week in Tucson, Arizona, in 1999.

At the invitation of a F/friend, the daughter of Buckminster Fuller of Geodesic Dome fame, I immersed myself in the week-long ceremony of Yaqui Easter. I knew almost nothing of the Yaqui, though as an anthropology major who had lived two years on the Rosebud (Lakota) Reservation, I had a deep and informed commitment to Indigenous beliefs and was yearning for ways of finding connection to universal love. I had come to appreciate the curious balance that many Native people have reached in their adoption of Christianity alongside   their own Indigenous faith traditions.

It is important to know that Christianity's darkest hours in America can be found in the "evil" treatment of Native peoples. Manifest Destiny and the Doctrine of Discovery are two of the most brutal episodes, not to mention the distribution of smallpox-infected blankets that led to the extermination of perhaps as many as 90% of Indigenous Americans.

Each Christian sect carries the blood on their hands and in their hearts of this slaughter of major proportions. The Doctrine of Discovery gave permission to kill anyone who was not Christian. Manifest Destiny said it was "by God's will" that the country was here for the Christian world and anyone else was not human and could be killed as any animal. These attitudes remained in place up to as recently as 1956, when children were still being killed by TB in the "charitable" boarding schools.

Catholics perhaps were the most brutal in their treatment of Native peoples. But the story is always more complicated. Not all Catholics, nor all Christians, were looking to destroy. And the story is that it was just such a Jesuit Priest (from Scotland) who came staggering out of the desert and found himself taken in by the Yaqui. This priest brought with him an innocence and home-sickness that was embraced by a people who were trying to rebuild their own world, and together they created what is called "Yaqui Easter."

The Yaqui Easter is the quintessential mix of the Indigenous beliefs of the Yaqui and the Catholic Easter celebration featuring the Stations of the Cross.

There is a 200-hour, live pageantry that begins with Lent. The week of Easter culminates with a nonstop march with as many as two hundred participating and thousands of observers coming together for "the Gloria."

The story of Easter is as you all know it, but the characters and symbolism are unique and powerful, with several additional characters and stories simultaneously in progress. It is these stories I wish to share. Not only do we have the major players of Jesus, Mary, the Disciples, the soldiers, the pharisees and the officialdom of the times. There are three other groups in the Yaqui version as well, and it is their stories that add to the Easter story in ways that are profound and bring this story of love, war, sacrifice and forgiveness to a new place from an ancient time.

There is a unique group of "clowns," people born with the gift of knowing the inner conflict of good and evil. They wear complex masks that represent the "evil" in the world, their behavior is "backward," and in their mouths they carry a backwards cross to protect them from the evil they themselves represent---war, plagues, starvation, and oppression.

There is the Deer Dancer and his musicians. They too come to this place from birth, born to the role. They represent the pre-Spanish time of preparing for the hunt. They represent the natural world that understands that they must be sacrificed for a people who cannot survive in good heart, good health and comfort without it.

And there is Mary. It is Mary who brings all from Calvary (the hill on which Judas is burned in effigy) to the hallowed ground as one body in the little church. She cuts through the bondage of each group, freeing them from their weapons, their false faces and gods---money, power, selfishness, oppression--- their "backward actions" and their disconnection from the "Good Heart." She brings them to "Gloria," whole, unfettered, supported as one entity. Her weapon kills not the man, but the false self.

Flowers are Mary's special weapon against evil. Mary's army is made of common people, women and children who bring song and flowers as their only weapons. It is these weapons of the "Good Heart" alone that can defeat the wrath and fear of the armed men. Flowers, particularly red flowers, represent the blessing of Mary throughout the year. It is red petals that fall, not blood, from Jesus on the cross.

It is after the third attempt to storm the little church where the pharisees think Jesus is hidden that the great Surrender to the Good Heart finally happens.

The dancers act out the story. (Here, at the UU, Emily read from a passage not available to us.) I remember how, on the third desperate rush to the little sanctuary, an old clown stumbles and a young soldier swoops down, lifts him and carries him to Glory.

I remember watching the children tying ribbons of red and pink, yellow and green to the arms of the soldiers as they throw their weapons on the fire. Then all of them together rush to HOME. They looked like birds, butterflies, joy.

I remember my own heart racing, the tears on my cheeks and the sense of---not salvation, not safety---but rest from the long, long struggle of playing their games, my games. HOME, bathed in light color and song, the peace of the world promised always, was here NOW. No better heaven could have been imagined. I took the joy offered and was grateful.

Does Race Matter?

January 2015

Does race matter? There is an answer we resist but know is true. Race matters more than any other factor in our world. We create the *them and us*, always. It is the ladder we climb up. It is the way we feel our place in the hierarchy of it all. Piri Thomas talked about the color spectrum in his own family: the lighter the better. He was the darkest and internalized the racism.

Race matters! LIFE matters! A Black Life Matters! A White Life Matters!

If you doubt it, stop for a moment and look again. The legacy of the white race has a horrific streak of blood that no washing seems to cleanse.

Fast forward through slavery, the Civil War, Jim Crow, the lynchings, the KKK, segregation, Civil Rights Movement, Voting Rights, MLK, Selma, Malcolm X, the penal system, the New Jim Crow in the name of justice. Whose justice?

Like the third strand of a braid, racism in America is as central as any other core belief we hold to be self-evident. Congress freed those in slavery in 1865, but not until 1965 were their descendants free to vote. Again today, fifty years after Selma, we are asked to look at the mentality of "them and us" that begins to again get our attention but is more of the same for African-Americans.

I have been grateful for a family tale that finds within my lineage both Native and African blood. It protects me from saying or even thinking "them and us."

It has been my very, very good fortune to be loved by two men who were African-American. They shared a life with me, and through that connection I saw the world as I had not imagined it before. I have seven bi-racial nieces and nephews and have felt the world of contradiction and stereotyping that I could not have known otherwise. I have heard the anguished cries of my brother and sisters as we compared the realities of our sons. I have felt the discrimination they and numerous others have faced. I have been embarrassed by my ushering them through the white man's world, myself a white, owning-class woman, entitled and privileged.

Walk in another's shoes and you see the world in ways that you have been pretending didn't exist. We have denied the injustice and felt that the curse is inherited and not ours to own. We blame the victim and they themselves internalize the racism. We imagine that they deserve what they get and we deserve what we get. Black and white, wrong and right. The dualism protects us from them and separates us, giving rise to the disconnect that flies in the face of the fundamental paradigm of all faith traditions: Do unto others.....

I was struck by the faith traditions of Barack Obama's mother, Stanley Ann Dunham. She was raised in a Unitarian congregation in Seattle, Washington, lived half her life with non-Christians in a Muslim world, spent time with unwed mothers, and studied a sacred craft long practiced exclusively by men. She is said to have wished for her children a life where they would come to know the world. She jokingly said a combination of Albert Einstein, Mahatma Gandhi and Harry Belafonte was what she wished her son to become. She never knew him to become president. She died at 55 of cancer.

I was sent an email this week by a young man which identified the children of the "Nones", (those who answer "none" to "What is your religion?") as having a strong and grounding ethic that is shared and universal. With little direction or coercion, it arises from the very same seed as the ethical systems of all faiths.

It is the Golden Rule that rises and that just might restore us to a world where justice is remembered, and vengeance is laid down.

(Here, Emily played, "a song from *Sweet Honey and the Rock,* a group of Black women who gathered to create a music that told of their lives, loves and losses.)

Black lives matter. We know this truth through the practice of our faith, in which we experience the spark of the Divine present in each of us. We know all persons to be equally worthy of love, respect, and justice. Tragically, fifty years after they were spoken, the words of famed civil rights organizer Ella Baker still apply: "Until the killing of black men, black mothers' sons, becomes as important to the rest of the country as the killing of a white mother's son, we who believe in freedom cannot rest." When we do not live out this truth, all of us are harmed, all of us are damaged.

All lives matter. But our civil society is constructed in a way that black and brown lives matter less than white lives. This condition extends beyond the matters of policing into education, the media, the system of mass incarceration, housing patterns, employment, and virtually every aspect of life in the United States, including its faith communities.

Therefore, we call for both recognition and remedy of this condition. We call upon civil authorities to take leadership in bringing about this recognition and remedy. We call upon all people of faith, ourselves included, to understand how we may be complicit in a system that extends privileges to people racialized as white, while denying the same to those racialized as people of color.

It is clearly in the interest of our shared humanity and our common spiritual condition to change these circumstances. It is in our material, economic, and social interests to do so as well. This is not easy work. But we pray the burden of this work may be easier to bear than the moral burden of settling back, once the current furor subsides, into complacent acceptance of a system and a society that fail to affirm our most fundamental relationships to God and to one another.

> *The idea whose time has come today is the idea of freedom and human dignity. All over the world we see signs of "the freedom explosion," and this reveals to us that we are in the midst of revolutionary times. An older order is passing away and a new order is coming into being...The role of the church [is] to broaden horizons, to challenge the status quo, and to question and break mores...The church has a major role to play in this period of social change...[It must] remain awake through this revolution.*
>
> *Source not stated*

Where are you looking for God?

January, year unknown

I am dedicating the lighting of the chalice today to the many indigenous elders around the world who have died and taken with them the truth of a knowing that we have no memory of. It is a wisdom I want to hold out as best I can, in deep gratitude for having been welcomed into a world few white people even know exists.

I asked you last week if you had heard yourselves calling upon God in this fractious and anxious time. I asked you what that meant to you, and who was God, where was God?

I have suggested before that for me, God is a verb, not a noun. God has been used to bring order into chaos and direction in a time of social collapse. God has been the handmaiden at both the rise and fall of civilizations.

God has been on our lips and in our cries of fear, cries for mercy and cries for salvation perhaps since forever. This mystery of which we are a part is unfathomable.

In these times many of us have not resonated with the litany. We have resisted subservience to religion but are becoming aware of the vast and miraculous power of the web of life of which we are a part.

My father, a doctor who found the deepest spiritual meaning in his role as witness at the bedside of his dying patients, called God the "Comforter." He called prayer a "sigh of surrender" to that which is beyond knowing.

No one I have known or accompanied in their dying who died consciously has called upon God, but certainly all appreciated the profound power of life as they hadn't known it until standing at the threshold; and only then, in a brief moment seeing with clarity both the life they had lived and the truth of the journey.

'Universal Knowing' is how my niece, who has stood on that threshold three, no, four times in her young life, describes it. A dear friend facing death spoke of "No seams, no them and us, now or then, right or wrong, black or white, good or bad." A Natural Habitat of One Whole that is held in a stasis that comforts, affirms and gives life. Yes, that is an essence of God that speaks to me.

When Einstein gave lectures at U.S. universities, the recurring question that students asked him most was, "Do you believe in God?"

And he always answered, "I believe in the God of Spinoza."

Baruch de Spinoza was a Dutch philosopher considered one of the great rationalists of 17th century philosophy, along with Descartes.

Spinoza spoke of a God who would say:

Stop praying.

What I want you to do is go out into the world and enjoy your life. I want you to sing, have fun and enjoy everything I've made for you.

Stop going into those dark, cold temples that you built yourself and saying they are my house. My house is in the mountains, in the woods, rivers, lakes, beaches. That's where I live and there, I express my love for you.

Stop blaming me for your miserable life; I never told you there was anything wrong with you or that you were a sinner, or that your sexuality was a bad thing. Sex is a gift I have given you and with which you can express your love, your ecstasy, your joy. So don't blame me for everything they made you believe.

Stop reading alleged sacred scriptures that have nothing to do with me. If you can't read me in a sunrise, in a landscape, in the look of your friends, in your son's eyes... you will find me in no book!

Stop asking me, "Will you tell me how to do my job?" Stop being so scared of me. I do not judge you or criticize you, nor get angry, or bothered. I am pure love.

Stop asking for forgiveness, there's nothing to forgive. If I made you... I filled you with passions, limitations, pleasures, feelings, needs, inconsistencies... free will. How can I blame you if you respond to something I put in you? How can I punish you for being the way you are, if I'm the one who made you? Do you think I could create a place to burn all my children who behave badly for the rest of eternity? What kind of god would do that?

Respect your peers and don't do what you don't want for yourself. All I ask is that you pay attention in your life, that alertness is your guide.

My beloved, this life is not a test, not a step on the way, not a rehearsal, nor a prelude to paradise. This life is the only thing here and now, and it is all you need.

I have set you absolutely free, no prizes or punishments, no sins or virtues, no one carries a marker, no one keeps a record.

You are absolutely free to create in your life heaven or hell.

I can't tell you if there's anything after this life, but I can give you a tip. Live as if there is not. As if this is your only chance to enjoy, to love, to exist. If there's nothing after, then you will have enjoyed the opportunity I gave you. And if there is, rest assured that I won't ask if you behaved right or wrong, I'll ask. Did you like it? Did you have fun? What did you enjoy the most? What did you learn?...

Stop believing in me; believing is assuming, guessing, imagining. I don't want you to believe in me, I want you to believe in you. I want you to feel me in you when you kiss your beloved, when you tuck in your little girl, when you caress your dog, when you bathe in the sea.

Stop praising me, what kind of egomaniac God do you think I am?

*I'm bored being praised. I'm tired of being
thanked. Feeling grateful? Prove it by taking
care of yourself, your health, your relationships,
the world. Express your joy! That's the way to
praise me.*

*Stop complicating things and repeating like a
parakeet what you've been taught about me.*

*What do you need more miracles for? So many
explanations?*

*The only thing for sure is that you are here, that
you are alive, that this world is full of wonders.*

Black Elk spoke and said:

*Teach me to walk the soft Earth as a relative to
all that live.*

Sweeten my heart and fill me with light.

Give me the strength to understand and the eyes

To see...

There is in these two wise men a quiet and stillness that feels alien to the frenetic pace that we identify with being alive. There is no "being in control" but just BEING. We seem to think that our actions and reactions are the measure of aliveness, but stand in the woods, resting with your back against a tree, and imagine the life of that tree among trees.

Let yourself feel yourself as water gathered from droplets of morning dew that slips from the leaves and petals and drops into a brook where at once it is no longer apart from the whole, but one with it. Let yourself feel the bonds which support but allow flexibility, rapids that with a buoyancy hold and carry you, a *you* that is both solitary and interconnected.

We as individuals and as a society need that clean water and healing sun and it's nurturing, so that the rigidity and isolation of our being can reclaim its humanity in the web of life.

In this time of rupture, division and unparalleled climate change, embedded in a legacy of injustice and colonization, our America has become too brittle, too disconnected to survive. It is no wonder that we cry out asking why we have been forsaken by God. Perhaps it is time to call forth a God of universal comfort manifested in the world as the living gift of life itself. Perhaps it is time to turn with gratitude for all this that God has provided.

For more and more of us, the God that we seek is in all and everything, and accessible with every breath, "if we have the eyes to see."

A poem by Chelan Harken speaks to my condition and brings me back to the place of comfort, balance and gratitude that I know is what I seek in my cry for God.

> *The worst thing we ever did*
>
> *was take the dance and the song*
>
> *out of prayer,*
>
> *make it sit up straight*
>
> *and cross its legs,*
>
> *remove it from rejoicing,*
>
> *wipe clean its hip sway,*

its questions,

its ecstatic yowl,

its tears.

The worst thing we ever did is pretend

God isn't the easiest thing

in this Universe

available to every soul

in every breath.

Three Minute Read*

March 2020

*Hello sweet one. I see how much you care about
the world, about your*

*communities, about all of us surviving plagues
and capitalism and a world on fire.*

*That clench in your throat, the knot in your gut,
the tightness in your breath — this is how our
bodies try to hold the world's anguish. We write
the wrongness into our bodies, a beautiful and
devastating lament.*

*Just because your body can hold all the tragedy,
the panic, the tension, that it is holding right
now, that doesn't mean that you must go on
holding it, all, forever. The loving grandmother
in you knows this to be true.*

*Set it down somewhere nearby, so you can pick it
up again when you need to; but just for a
moment, relinquish your illusions of control.
Allow yourself to see the many-headed Truth
monster: things might not all be okay. They might*

end in flames and death and horror, no matter what you do. Take a moment to acknowledge how fucking awful and sad that Truth is. And how not even the worst possible scenario would take away from your inherent worthiness.

Simultaneously, it is True that human beings have always fought for one another, cared for one another fiercely, and carried the world's anguish in our bodies. And there are small Truths, like that we cannot control the future, no matter how much we wish we could. (Don't worry when the Truths contradict one another, real Truths often do.)

No matter what, whether it turns out okay in the end or not, you carry the Divine within you. You are Enough, not because of the things you do but because of who you are fundamentally. Intrinsically. Always and without exception. Take a breath or two to allow yourself to Know this.

And when we pick up the anxiety again, let us aim for flexibility. Movement space for breath to get in and out of your rib cage, gentleness for the things we can't do, and Integrity giving us the strength and resolve to turn our sometimes-

excruciating caring into solidarity, mutual aid, and direct action.

We are each one person, breathing this one breath, with common Divinity.

We can do this. Together.

*Note: This poem was an email response from my therapist when she closed her office because of coronavirus. The author has given permission for *YES! Magazine* to publish it but wishes to remain anonymous. —Ayu Sutriasa

Indigenous Peoples' Prayer

At the end of one of her talks at AFSI, Emily shared a prayer of the Indigenous Peoples.

Oh, Great Spirit, whose voice I hear in the wind and whose breath gives life to all the world, hear me. I am small and weak, and I need your strength and wisdom.

Let me walk in beauty and make my eyes ever behold the red and purple sunset. Make my hands respect the things you made, and my ears sharp to your voice.

Make me wise so that I may understand the things you have taught my people. Let me learn the lessons you have hidden in every rock and every leaf.

I seek strength, not to be greater that my brother or my sister, but to fight my greatest enemy, myself.

Make me always ready to come to you with clean hands and straight eyes, so that when life fades as the fading sunset, my spirit, my spirit may come to you without shame.

68675374R00089